N

Encouraging Physical Activity in Preschoolers

Moving Matters Series

Steve Sanders, EdD

Gryphon House
www.gryphonhouse.com

Published by Gryphon House, Inc.
P. O. Box 10, Lewisville, NC 27023
800.638.0928; 877.638.7576 (fax)
Visit us on the web at www.gryphonhouse.com.

Bulk Purchase

Gryphon House books are available for special premiums and sales promotions as well as for fund-raising use. Special editions or book excerpts also can be created to specifications. For details, call 800.638.0928.

Disclaimer

Library of Congress Cataloging-in-Publication Data

The Cataloging-in-Publication Data is registered with the Library of Congress for ISBN: 978-0-87659-046-1.

Contents

The Importance of Physical Activity for Preschoolers

CHAPTER

1

Whether you are a teacher, a home-based caregiver, or a parent, by helping preschool children discover their capabilities and reach their potential through physical activity, you are serving as their guide on a remarkable journey. Over the next several years, the preschool children in your care will develop and refine a variety of motor skills that they will use throughout life to be physically active and remain healthy. You may be wondering what qualifies as physical activity. Many health and fitness organizations categorize it as any body movement that results in energy expenditure above resting. Therefore, any movement a child does other than sitting or lying down can be considered physical activity. However, we will focus on activity levels that improve health and physical development. Along with caregivers, parents serve as an important resource in helping preschool children develop their physical skills. Your role is to play with the children, provide appropriate activity equipment, and help guide them to learn about their physical potential.

You might be thinking, "I am not very physically skilled. Will I be able to teach a child how to jump, balance, throw, catch, or kick a ball?" The answer is that you do not have to be skilled to help children develop a foundation of physical skills; all you have to do is participate in the adventure. The activities in this book are simple and straightforward and do not require you to be a professional athlete or a trained physical-education teacher. You can help children develop motor skills! This is going to be fun and exciting for you and the children in your care.

If you want children to reach their potential to be physically active throughout life, the preschool years are a crucial time. This is the time when basic physical or motor skills are developed. Just like learning to write, read, or understand numbers, learning motor skills is essential to learning about the world. As children grow, having a foundation of physical skills will enable them to participate in all kinds of fun activities. The basic motor skills discussed in this book include those related to traveling (moving from one place to another), balancing, jumping, throwing, catching, kicking, striking with body parts, striking with rackets, and striking with long-handled implements.

Adults participate in physical activity and maintain fitness and health through skill-based activities such as dance, tennis, swimming, golf, basketball, aerobics, walking, and bicycling. If children feel competent in many motor skills, they will have a greater tendency to participate in physical activity later as adults. Physical skill development is at the center of young children's physical growth. No matter what the activity, a child cannot take part successfully if he has not mastered the essential fundamental movement skills contained within that activity. Therefore, if children are going to lead physically active and healthy lives, now and as adults, a foundation of physical skills must be developed. This approach is grounded in the knowledge that children who have not developed a foundation of physical skills become adults who typically do not participate in physical activity.

Physical skills take time to learn and require practice to refine. Although all children have the potential to develop these skills, many do not receive opportunities to learn the basics. Without a foundation of skills, they quickly can become turned off to physical activity. Children who have difficulty with gross-motor activities may experience frustration and poor self-esteem. Some children who find motor skills challenging will avoid participation because they fear failure. These children will then have fewer opportunities to practice and improve their physical skills.

By helping a preschool child embark on this physical-skill adventure, you will ensure that by the time he is six and entering school, he will have a strong foundation and will feel confident in his ability to run, jump, skip, and gallop. He will know the basic techniques involved when balancing, kicking, throwing, catching, dribbling, volleying, and striking with rackets and bats. Most of all, the development of these basic skills will provide the opportunity to refine physical skills in a variety of games and physical activities throughout the elementary years and throughout life.

The intent here is not to make children into professional athletes; you are simply teaching them the basics and providing guidelines as they work to develop essential physical skills. Each child will develop motor skills at his own pace, and all children will demonstrate different strengths and abilities depending on their interests. Having the skills to read, write, and do math helps children understand how the world works. Similarly, having the skills to balance, throw, catch, and kick a ball helps children understand how to interact with others and carve out a comfortable place in the physical world. When you work with children to develop a foundation of the basic physical skills, you prepare them to participate with confidence in any physical-activity opportunity that may come along. Above all, the purpose is for both of you to enjoy moving and playing together. For physical activity to become an important part of a child's life, it must be fun!

The information provided here will help you explore the importance of physical development, considerations for setting up an environment that promotes physical activity, the types of equipment you will need, and strategies for presenting learning activities to children. The physical-skills section defines and presents the essential skills and is full of activities for caregivers, children, and families to do in the learning environment or at home. Join with other adults and children, and get started moving and learning in your center's play area, in a nearby park, or in your own backyard. Play and be physically active with the preschoolers in your care as much as you can. Having a foundation of physical skills helps children make friends, develop confidence, and participate in daily physical activity. Regularly using these skills will also help decrease the child's risk for many illnesses and will help improve the child's overall health.

Keep in mind that this book is promoting higher-level activities, not movements such as walking across the yard to get into the car, strolling across the room to turn on the TV, or sitting at a table eating a meal. Although all of these are low-level forms of physical activity, participation will not improve health. The discussion will focus on physical activity that is above what you normally do just to move through the day. Some examples of healthy physical activity might include walking, biking, climbing, dancing, gardening, swimming, and all kinds of games involving skills such as throwing, catching, kicking, and striking. These movements burn calories, work the muscles, and increase the heart rate.

As you know, preschool children are physically active from the time they get up in the morning to when they go to bed at night. Most people who care for preschoolers cannot imagine these children being more active. What educators know from research and experience is that many children will participate less and less in physical activity as they get older. This decrease stems from many factors, but one of the top reasons is that many children do not develop the foundation of skills they need to participate.

ACTIVITY LEVELS— DID YOU KNOW?

Preschoolers are in constant motion, but this is not the case with many older children. Participation in all types of physical activity declines strikingly as age or grade in school increases. Research suggests that older adolescents are less likely than younger children to be physically active, and adolescent girls are less likely than their male peers to be physically active. Nearly half of U.S. youths twelve to twenty-one years old are not vigorously active on a regular basis. However, young people who believe they are competent and have physical skills are more likely to be active regularly.

Many physical activities do not require a high level of skill to participate. Walking, for example, does not require much skill. Galloping, skipping, balancing, jumping, throwing, catching, kicking, and striking with paddles and bats are more complicated. They will require practice with the necessary skills and assistance from adults to master them. Learning about and participating in physical activity is similar to learning to read a book—you need a foundation of skills to do both. To read, a child must understand what letters are, that letters form words, and that words form sentences. As the child grows, she will learn about verbs, nouns, adverbs, and punctuation. She will develop the knowledge and obtain the skills needed to read. Likewise, a preschool child will need to learn the basic skills required for participating in physical activity.

Preschool-age children who are capable of walking unaided should be physically active daily for at least 180 minutes (three hours), including activity that makes them huff and puff. This activity does not have to be done all at once. It can be built up throughout the day in fifteen- to twenty-minute segments. As well as encouraging physical activity, limit the amount of time that children under five years of age spend watching television, using small-screen devices, or playing on the computer to two hours a day or less.

Promoting a Healthy Lifestyle

Physical activity is essential at all ages, but it is especially important for the preschool child. Research suggests that the key to helping a child be physically active is discovering activities that the child finds fun and feels successful doing. Children and many adults may shy away from physical activity if they are insecure about their abilities. Therefore, in addition to enjoying the activity and having fun, it is important for children to develop and improve the fundamental motor skills needed to participate in a variety of physical activities.

You can help make physical activity a priority by scheduling opportunities for children to play. Having regular play time encourages children to develop good habits and practice the skills they will need to continue to be active for many years to come. Learning and refining motor skills during physical activity permits children to fully explore and function in their environment and supports their social and cognitive development.

Many different forms of physical activity are possible, but not all of them benefit children in the same way. Research has found that children who spend the most time in moderate-to-vigorous physical activity tend to have the highest levels of motor skills. This may be because physically active children spend more time learning and improving new motor skills. Children with better motor skills may also find physical activity easier and more fun. Here are some visible signs that can indicate the intensity of a child's physical activity:

- **Sedentary:** not participating in any physical movement (watching TV, reading, drawing, taking naps)
- **Light:** not out of breath (moving about, standing up, walking at a slow pace)
- **Moderate to vigorous:** heart is beating fast; may be out of breath (running, swimming, biking)

A number of sources, including the American Academy of Pediatrics, the American Medical Association, and the U.S. Department of Health and Human Services, have summarized the research findings on the rewards of regular physical activity. Here are some of the benefits for children:

- Physical activity strengthens the heart. The heart is an organ consisting of muscle. Like other muscles, the heart's performance improves when it is regularly challenged. The heart responds to physical activity by becoming stronger and more efficient.
- Physical exertion helps keep arteries and veins clear. Exercise reduces the amount of harmful cholesterol and fats in a person's blood. It

increases the flexibility of the walls of blood vessels and helps to lower blood pressure.

- High levels of activity can strengthen the lungs. As the child increases her movement and becomes more and more active, she increases lung capacity. The lungs then become more efficient in moving air in and out of the body. As a result, more oxygen is drawn into the body, and more carbon dioxide and other waste gases are expelled.

- Physical activity reduces blood-sugar levels. Exercise prevents sugar from accumulating in the blood by triggering muscles to take up more glucose (sugar) from the bloodstream and use it for energy. This can reduce a person's risk of developing diabetes.

- Being active can control weight gain. When a child is sedentary and spends much of the day sitting, she tends to take in more calories than she needs. These unused calories accumulate as fat. A child who is physically active uses more calories, which takes fat away and lowers weight. Lowered weight is good for the child's heart.

- Physical activities can improve bone density and strength, which may lead to improved posture for children. All that jumping preschoolers do is great for building stronger bones.

- Regular physical activity often makes children feel more energetic and reduces the likelihood that they will tire during the day.

- When a child is physically active—using up large amounts of energy and calories during the day—he sleeps better at night.

- Active movement enhances emotional well-being. Most adults report that they feel calmer and happier after they are physically active. This also can be true for children, as physical activity releases beta-endorphin, a natural substance in the body associated with feelings of well-being, heightening of appetite, and lessening of mental depression.

- Active children tend to perform better in school. Physical exertion increases oxygen flow to the brain and directly affects brain behavior and development. The Centers for Disease Control (CDC) report titled *Health and Academic Achievement* suggests that physical activity can positively affect cognitive skills and attitudes and behavior in the learning environment, all of which are important components

Sleep is directly related to physical activity and is essential to children's health. Experts recommend ten to twelve hours of sleep per day for children ages three to six. Rest is as important as physical activity for healthy growth and development. Research suggests that children who spend time in vigorous physical activity are quicker to fall asleep and sleep longer. Children who exercise less during the day take longer to fall asleep at night.

of improved academic performance. These include enhanced concentration, attention, and on-task behavior.

Children who are not physically active enough will not have the chance to get these benefits and are at increased risk of becoming overweight or obese. Weight gain in turn makes it harder for them to be active and keep up with others, either in sport or in play. Active children typically become active grown-ups. By encouraging children to be physically active, you are helping them set up healthy lifelong habits.

Risks: Overweight and Obese Children

In addition to knowing the benefits of daily physical activity for children, it is also important to provide information related to lack of physical activity. Media coverage has provided statistics on the alarming rise of childhood and adult obesity. Despite all the attention, the problem is not improving. Overweight and obese children are more likely to be victims of bullying, be sick more often than their normal-weight peers, develop sleep apnea, and become obese adults. Research suggests that more than 50 percent of children who are overweight or obese between the ages of three and six are still overweight or obese at age twenty-five.

About one in three children and adolescents in the United States was overweight or obese in 2012, according to the CDC's *Childhood Obesity Facts*. By keeping active, children are less likely to become overweight in the first place or to become overweight during later stages of life, according to *Physical Activity Facts* from the CDC. So you can help them stay healthy and have a good body image by encouraging active movement.

Obesity among children has reached epidemic levels. Although there are a lot of reasons for this increase in childhood obesity, the number one reason children become overweight is the lack of daily physical activity. That, combined with poor eating habits and increased time spent watching television or playing video games, has helped to create a culture of overweight and obese children.

Parents and caregivers must grasp the concept that the quality of children's lives, now and in the future, depends partially on empowering them to participate daily in physical activity. Children are less active now than at any point in history. One in three children is overweight or obese. They eat more fast food than their parents did and interact outdoors far less than young people did twenty years ago. One in four children eats fast food each day. On average, children now spend more than 7.5 hours each day in front of a TV, according to the President's Council on Fitness, Sports and Nutrition. Certainly the U.S. culture is changing, and the consequence of this trend is increased frequency of overweight and obese children.

This problem is not going away. But you can help by taking steps to help children maintain an appropriate weight and increase their levels of daily physical activity. The benefits are healthy bodies, healthy self-esteem, and healthy lifestyles.

Understanding Motor Development

Learning can be defined as a permanent change in behavior resulting from experience and practice. *Motor development* is the process of change in a child's movement abilities related to physical skills involved with locomotion (running, galloping, and skipping), manipulation (throwing, catching, and striking), and stability (jumping and landing, and balance). Many factors can affect motor-skill development. The information in this book prepares you to help children learn the fundamental movement or motor patterns needed to perform a variety of physical skills.

You will find examples of experiences and practice activities that will help children learn a new motor pattern or skill. After practice over a period of time, the skills will become more and more automatic, and you will see a permanent change in the child's ability to perform these skills.

A position statement from the National Association for Sport and Physical Education (NASPE), *Looking at Physical Education from a Developmental Perspective,* observes that motor development is an interactional process leading to changes in behavior over time. This document outlines some simple principles related to developmental changes in children as they learn physical skills. (For further information, NASPE is now known as Shape America, and the position statement is available on the organization's website.) Understanding the principles of motor development will help you create a positive learning environment where physical skills can be practiced and mastered.

Different Rates of Development

First, a critical premise of motor-skill development is that children develop at different rates. Some kindergarten children can skip; others may not skip until they are in second or third grade. Some three-year-olds are able to track a ball in motion; others may be five or six before they obtain this skill.

Be patient as you work with preschoolers, as it may take years for a particular child to develop a mature kicking, throwing, or striking pattern. While one child is inconsistent in throwing ability, the child's younger friend might already be able to demonstrate a mature throwing pattern. A child is not behind in motor development if he cannot strike a ball with a bat at age five. In fact, most children do not develop a mature form of striking with a bat until later in elementary school. So it is not helpful to compare all children at the same age.

Change is individual. The general sequence of change remains the same for everyone, but the rate of change differs from one child to another. Change results from a multitude of factors that come together in different ways and at different times for different individuals. It occurs in the context of an individual child's body characteristics, environmental surroundings, and opportunities to practice physical skills.

Development is related to a child's age but is not determined by it. Many three-year-olds can gallop, but simply being a three-year-old does not mean a child will gallop. Many preschools will provide developmental charts suggesting that children should have certain skills at a specific age. This information is simply a developmental benchmark. Some children reach the benchmark early, and some do not meet the benchmark until much later.

Age simply does not predict motor ability. If it did, then all adults would be skilled athletes. Although there are certain advantages as children grow older (quicker reflexes and better visual-tracking ability), the only way individuals become adept with motor skills is to use, or practice, those skills. Thus most adults are reasonably efficient at walking. Many, however, are inefficient at catching a ball or striking an object with a racket. They are inefficient not because they lack the potential to be skillful but because they have not used the skills regularly over a period of years and have not developed the fundamental motor patterns.

Changes in motor skills happen sequentially over time. Children crawl before they walk, and they walk before they run. Their motor skills develop in an orderly manner. The important thing to remember is that children can advance in all skills from an immature stage to an advanced stage with practice.

Developmental change is cumulative. Early behaviors act as building blocks for later emerging skills.
For example:

- Running is built on walking.
- Catching a small ball is built on first catching larger balls.
- Running to kick a ball into a net is built on first making contact with a stationary ball.

Single factors do not cause developmental change; rather, it results from many factors acting together. A child can jump from both feet at the same time and land on two feet when he has the strength, balance, and motivation to do so. The emergence of the two-footed jump is not the result of any one of these factors but the result of interactions among all of them. The rate of a child's change may be limited by a lack of progress in one or more areas.

Myths about Motor Development

Before moving on to discuss how principles of motor development can help you design an environment for skill practice, there are some myths about motor-skill development that you should be aware of.

The first myth is that children can develop motor skills through play. Play is used for understanding the physical and social world; skill development does not just naturally happen through play. There is certainly evidence that motor skills may develop through informal play (for example, hours of basketball or soccer practice), but children need more than just play time to develop physical skills. They need help from their peers and from knowledgeable adults to develop and refine a foundation of physical skills. However, when children play on the playground or in the backyard, they can further practice and refine skills taught by caregivers and parents. Children do not learn to read by picking up a book and looking at the pictures. They need adults to help them understand what letters and words mean. Then they can practice reading books and refine their reading skills. Motor skills are developed in much the same way. Children practice individual parts of a skill, sometimes with instruction from an adult, and then they practice and refine the skill during play time. Giving children play and practice time is critically important. Children who spend lots of time in low-level activities, in front of the TV, or playing video games do not get the opportunities other children have to practice skills; therefore, they do not tend to participate in healthy physical activity as they grow older.

A second myth about motor development and skill acquisition relates to the idea of the natural athlete. Although some children are genetically disposed to do better at some sports or physical activities than others, the fact is that most highly skilled children have participated in one or many sports from very early ages. Some children begin kindergarten with mature throwing and catching patterns, for example. They played a lot of catch with parents, caregivers, siblings, or friends from a young age and thus enter school more highly skilled than their peers. In time, their less-skilled peers can catch up if they, too, practice and use the motor skill thousands of times as they play with friends, on teams, or with caregivers or parents. Motor development is not automatic. If children are to develop physical competence, they need a variety of equipment and materials; planned, appropriate movement experiences; and opportunities to practice and apply previously learned skills.

Developmentally Appropriate Practice

The term *developmentally appropriate practice* suggests that caregivers are presenting physical-skill activities and instruction to children using methods that will benefit and enhance the children's ability to learn new skills. If you are using information based on research and experience about how children grow and develop, you are more likely to understand best practices and successfully tailor instruction to children.

Developmentally appropriate practices include those that are both age appropriate and individually appropriate. Age-appropriate activity suggests that the child is at an age that is developmentally appropriate

to begin learning a skill via the activity. For example, most preschool children are developmentally ready to practice bouncing a ball, so that activity would be considered age appropriate for a preschool child. If you placed a child on a basketball team at age four and she was not yet competent in bouncing a ball, this would be considered a developmentally inappropriate activity. It would be inappropriate because the child does not yet have the skills to participate in the game.

When providing skill-development activities, you need to be aware if the child is individually ready for the activity. Some children can handle specific challenges before others. For example, most four-year-old children are not yet ready to continuously swing a rope and jump. But some four-year-olds can swing a rope and jump several times in a row. You will have to observe and make a judgment on when a child is ready for certain activities and when it is best to wait. You do not want to push children to practice skills if they are not developmentally ready for them, but you also do not want to hold them back if they are ready to learn. There is no magic formula for knowing when to introduce skills; it all depends on the developmental level of the particular child.

For an activity to be developmentally appropriate, it also should be instructionally appropriate. In other words, you should provide a fitting environment for learning new skills and should present tasks and activities to children in suitable ways. The following instructional practices will help you establish a positive physical-activity environment:

- Children learn through involvement, observation, and modeling. Construct the environment with specific skill learning in mind, and then guide the children toward learning the skills. By carefully observing a child's responses and interests, you can adapt the learning experiences to meet the needs of that child.

- Children should be allowed to seek creative solutions. Give them time and opportunities to explore appropriate responses.

- Parents should show interest and participate in skill-development activities. They are their children's first role models and most relied-on source for information.

- Children need a variety of experiences to help them obtain a mature level of fundamental motor skills. Select activities that are at the appropriate ability level for that child. Do not push activities just because you think they might be fun or because other children can already do the activities.

- Children should be able to make choices and explore what their bodies can do. Always provide them with opportunities to play with equipment and experiment before you provide any instruction on how to do a skill better.

- Provide a variety of different sizes, shapes, and weights of equipment. All equipment should match the developmental level of the child. A basketball or softball would be inappropriate for a preschool child to bounce or throw. The items are just too heavy for a small child to be successful with them. Modify equipment when appropriate, such as using a punch-ball balloon to strike instead of a ball.

- Repetition during practice is important to learning new skills. For example, challenge children to throw and hit a target ten times in a row so they can work on developing the desired throwing movement pattern.

- Children will not develop a solid foundation of physical skills without frequent practice. Practicing a skill one or two times is not enough. With repetition of all skills, they can develop a broad base of strong skills.

- When learning new skills, competition with others delays the developmental process. Activities should emphasize self-improvement instead of winning and losing. Competing against oneself is developmentally appropriate for preschool children, but competing against others is not.

- Young children learn best when they are successful. Make sure activities provide children with challenges and opportunities to practice skills at high rates of success.

In 1994, the Council on Physical Education for Children created a set of guidelines specifically to help caregivers understand developmental issues related to preschool physical development. Understanding these issues can help child care–center, preschool, and kindergarten teachers to provide physical-activity programs that will best benefit children. When parents begin the process of selecting a preschool for their child, they should ask if the center provides a developmentally appropriate physical-activity program.

Caregivers and directors should also assess whether their program provides developmentally appropriate activities. The following questions can help.

- Do you have both indoor and outdoor spaces for physical activity? Are the spaces safe? Are physical activities restricted due to a lack of space?

- Does the program have a written physical-activity curriculum? Does the curriculum focus on development of basic skills? A curriculum loaded with games emphasizing rules and formations would be considered inappropriate for preschool children. Curriculum goals should emphasize development of basic skills.

- Does the curriculum emphasize fitness activities? Preschool children get their fitness through participation in skill-development activities. They are not developmentally ready to participate in adult fitness activities. Running laps, doing calisthenics, and following recorded aerobics programs, which set expectations that all children move in time with the music and do the same things at the same time, are definitely not appropriate.

- Do children have opportunities to be involved and remain active? Activities where children are waiting in lines for a turn in relay races, to be chosen for a team, or because of limited equipment would be considered developmentally inappropriate. Games in which a child is eliminated from playing also would be inappropriate.

- Is physical instruction built into the daily schedule in addition to free play and recess?
- What is the class size during physical activity? Is more than one academic classroom put together for physical activity? Group size should be limited to no more than twenty four- or five-year-olds with two adults. Younger children require smaller groups.
- Is there enough physical-skill-development equipment available for all children in a class? Children should not have to wait in lines to use equipment.
- Is equipment sized for children? Adult-size equipment may inhibit skill development, or may injure or intimidate children.
- Are caregivers trained to help children develop physical skills?

Physically Active with Special Needs

All children, including those with differences in mental or physical ability, have the need to develop physical skills and be physically active. All children have unique needs, and you can help by modifying activities to meet those special needs.

Children with disabilities tend to be less physically active than children without disabilities. Yet they need physical activity to develop skills for recreational use throughout life. Physical activity improves health. Increased physical activity brings increased muscle tone and strength, especially for those prone to being less mobile. Skill development is just as important f or a preschool child with a disability as it is for a child who reaches physical milestones when developmentally expected.

The purpose here is not to discuss all the disabilities that children may face but to give g eneral direction on how you might help children with disabilities develop physical skills. Children with special needs should strive to develop the same physical skills as other children if possible. What may be different is the way you present activities to the children and the adaptations you make to teach the skills. A particular child may not be able to fully develop all the basic physical skills. If this is the case, select the physical skills that can be developed and that the child shows interest in, then emphasize those skills.

All children will require instruction, repetition, and practice to develop motor skills. Physical skills do

not develop in exactly the same way for all preschoolers. Although some variation is normal, children with disabilities may need even more time and instruction. Consider the following strategies that may further help in teaching a child with a disability:

- Present the tasks at the child's level of functioning. If the task is too difficult, break the task into smaller steps.

- Remove distractions such as extra equipment. To avoid cluttering the environment, have available only the specific equipment needed for the task at hand.

- Develop a daily schedule or routine and use it.

- Provide more feedback that is task specific, such as, "I like the way you use your fingertips when bouncing the ball." Demonstrate skills whenever possible.

- Emphasize the child's abilities rather than disabilities. Stay away from activities that may be frustrating, and try them again when the child shows interest in learning the skill.

- Select skills that are functional for the child, such as throwing (or dropping) a ball into a large basket as opposed to trying to hit a target that is on a wall.

- Provide children with more frequent opportunities to practice so they can retain the skill levels they have achieved.

Encouraging Physical Activity in Preschoolers

- Increase the size of the target when throwing or kicking (make the target larger or the goal wider), and experiment with different sizes of balls until you find one that best suits the child's needs. Reduce the weight or size of the striking implement, such as using a lighter bat to practice striking or using a foam ball to throw or catch.
- Strike off a tee instead of tossing a ball to the child.
- Always work at ground level with balance activities (use a balance beam that is only a few inches off the ground), and let the child develop some proficiency before moving to a beam that is at a higher level.
- Ask a child with a visual impairment to hold your hand during travel practice or to touch the shoulder of a preschool friend who is moving directly in front of him. Use oral cues to tell the child what to do.
- Play follow-the-leader games by asking a child with a visual impairment to hold a short rope as you lead him slowly by holding the other end of the rope. Use your hands to adjust the child's body parts to ensure the correct positions.
- When providing instruction to a child with a hearing impairment, always demonstrate the skill at the same time and provide the child opportunities to watch others whenever possible.

IDEA— DID YOU KNOW?

Every child with a disability is required to receive instruction in physical education, even if all other students in the preschool do not receive such instruction. The Individuals with Disabilities Education Act (IDEA) provides that a child between the ages of three and nine may be considered disabled if the child is experiencing developmental delays in physical, cognitive, communication, or social or emotional development. When a child begins school, parents should notify the school administration of the physical disability and the child's needs. According to IDEA, school staff must work with the family to provide age-appropriate physical-skill instruction.

Importance of Physical Play

Besides instruction and practice, physical play is also important in promoting skill development and physical activity. Overall, play is important because it contributes to children's cognitive, social, emotional, and physical growth. It also provides opportunities for caregivers and parents to engage daily with the children. Children are naturally playful and will usually join in when given an opportunity. Play lets children explore, discover, and try to make sense out of the world.

During physical play, children have time to explore, manipulate objects, and practice physical skills on their own. Physical play helps them learn how to use their muscles. Muscles get stronger and work better when children exercise them. Children need lots of opportunities to develop upper-body strength and confidence by climbing and hanging from playground equipment, striking balls with paddles, and throwing bean bags at targets. They also will need opportunities to strengthen the lower body by jumping up and down, balancing on one foot, and kicking a ball across a field. If children do not have enough chances to kick, throw, catch, jump, and balance, their muscles will not be as strong and they will not be as skilled as children who do have these play experiences.

Play, which cannot be structured for a child, is easier to recognize than it is to define. When you introduce a child to the skills of throwing, kicking, or balancing, you might call those activities play. However, you are in charge and are giving the child feedback about learning the new skill, so it is really instruction time. Play has no adult instructions; it is voluntary and fun. With play, the child is choosing and directing the activities. You can follow along and play with the children, but this is not instruction time. Children should enjoy play time in addition to instruction time. Physical play is practice time, a time for children to practice and refine skills they have been working on with your guidance. It is also time for children to explore, experiment, and learn new things on their own.

For children to develop a base of physical skills, they will need opportunities for adult instruction and for play. Play alone may not provide children with a foundation of skills, but it can provide them with opportunities to practice and refine skills that are introduced by caregivers and parents. Play is important because it helps children gain a sense of mastery and competency of skills. When a child throws a ball and hits a target, walks across a balance beam without falling, or kicks a ball into a net, all without adult help, these play activities will really add to her sense of confidence in her physical abilities.

Technology in the form of television, video games, and cell phones has an effect on physical play and should be limited during the preschool years. Times are changing. Although playing with technology (passive play) can have some benefits, most of today's electronic devices did not exist twenty years ago, when preschool children spent most of their time physically playing and interacting with others. Many children now are learning computer skills before they learn basic physical skills. In a 2014 survey, AVG, an online security company, found that more three- to five-year-olds could play a computer game (66 percent) than could ride a bike (58 percent). Similarly, the study found that more of the children could navigate a tablet or smartphone (47 percent) than could swim unaided (23 percent). About four times as many children ages three to five could play with an application for a connected device (57 percent) than could tie their shoelaces (14 percent). To promote physical-skill development, limit passive play to about 20 percent of play time, and expand physical play to about 80 percent of the time allowed.

Shape America has recommended that all children be involved in at least sixty minutes of physical activity each day, including play time. This time does not have to be continuous but can be broken into smaller chunks of time, for example, twenty-minute periods three times a day.

To ensure that children have enough play time, preschool programs should have daily recess, which gives children time to play with friends and practice physical and social skills. In an environment where test scores rule education policy, many schools have significantly reduced or completely cut recess time. Recess breaks should be scheduled at least every two hours in an all-day preschool to provide opportunities to rest from inside academic activities and to practice positive social skills with peers. Recess should be a period of free, unstructured play.

There is plenty of evidence that recess (unstructured play) benefits children in cognitive, social-emotional, and physical ways. Research suggests that when children have recess, they show the following characteristics:

- More on task in the classroom
- Improved memory and more focused attention
- More likely to take turns, demonstrate leadership, and learn to resolve conflicts
- More physically active before and after school

Nutritional Awareness

Why is there a section on nutritional awareness in a book about children's physical activity? Physical activity and nutrition behaviors are closely linked, and it is important for caregivers and children to be aware of some basic information on the relationship between healthy eating habits and physical activity. Three important nutritional areas directly relate to physical activity—energy balance, body mass index, and liquids and hydration.

Striving for Energy Balance

Any discussion of physical activity in the life of a preschool child should begin with the concept of energy balance. Children need energy every day to play, be active, and grow normally. Energy comes from food and drink. All foods provide energy, but some provide more than others. The key is for children to balance the energy they take in with the energy used. Some children might find this easy because they are growing rapidly and are always on the go. For others who may not be as active or who consume too many of the wrong kinds of calories each day, it might not be so easy.

Everything we do uses energy. Breathing, sleeping, growing, and even thinking use some energy. Other activities children might participate in, such as running, jumping, kicking, swimming, or climbing on the playground, use a lot of energy. Different activitities use different amounts of energy. *Energy* is just another word for calories. Scientists find out how much energy there is in a food or drink by burning a sample of it and measuring how much heat is released. Labels on most foods provide information on the number of calories included per serving.

To be healthy and maintain a healthy weight, children (and adults) must balance the energy they take in as food with the energy they use being active and growing. What children eat and drink is energy in, and what they burn through physical activity and growing is energy out. For a child to maintain a healthy weight, he needs to balance the amount of energy he takes in (food and drink) with the energy he uses by being active. If

Encouraging Physical Activity in Preschoolers

a child takes in more energy than his body burns up, he will get out of balance and start to store this extra energy as excess fat. If a child begins to gain excessive weight, it may be because the amount of energy he is taking in is more than the amount he is using.

A healthy diet for preschool children should aim to balance the amount of energy and nutrients a child takes in with the amount of physical activity the child participates in each day. Eating foods that have a lot of nutrients and fewer calories, such as fruits, vegetables, and whole grains, helps keep the amount of calories low. If children consume foods or drinks that have large amounts of sugar, they will take in more calories and can get out of energy balance.

Keep in mind that energy in and energy out do not have to balance every day. Having a balance over time, however, will help children stay at a healthy weight for the long term. Energy balance in children happens when energy in and energy out support natural growth without promoting excess weight gain.

All of the energy, or calories, a child takes in each day is not used just for being physically active. A child's body uses energy from food and drinks to fuel basic functions such as breathing, pumping blood, digestion, maintaining body temperature, and growing. These activities take up between 45 and 70 percent of a child's total energy expenditure, depending on factors such as weight, height, and physical-activity level. The remaining 30 to 55 percent is used for physical activity.

DAILY CALORIES

It is important to know the number of calories a child needs to eat each day to stay healthy. Most preschool children should have a daily calorie intake of between 1400 and 1600 calories. If a child is extremely active, 200 to 400 extra calories may be needed.

Healthy Weight and BMI

Most pediatricians collect body mass index (BMI) data for preschoolers. The American Academy of Pediatrics recommends BMI screenings for all children age two years and older. As children grow and their bodies change, it is not always easy to tell if a child falls within a healthy weight range.

BMI estimates how much body fat a child may have. In simple terms, it measures a child's body shape based on weight and height. During the child's annual physical, the doctor will determine the child's height and weight and then calculate the child's BMI. Based on this calculation, the doctor can then determine if the child is underweight, at a healthy weight, overweight, or obese. Overweight or obese children are not in balance with energy in and energy out. If a child falls into those ranges, parents should talk with the child's pediatrician about providing a diet with fewer calories or providing more physical activity.

BMI, when looked at over time, can provide useful insight for parents and doctors to assess whether a child's weight is progressing in a healthy pattern related to age and gender. However, BMI calculations are not as accurate for children as they are for adults. Children's body-fat percentages change as they grow, and BMI scores may vary based on age and gender. The important point is that a child's BMI can help determine if she is at risk for health problems based on her weight, if she has the most appropriate diet, and if she is getting enough physical activity.

WEIGHT GAIN— DID YOU KNOW?

If a child eats just 150 calories more a day than she burns, this can lead to an extra 5 pounds over six months. That is a gain of 10 pounds a year. If you do not want this weight gain to happen, you can either reduce the child's energy in or increase the child's energy out.

CALCULATING BMI

If you are interested in calculating BMI, the formula is the child's weight in pounds divided by height in inches squared and then multiplied by 703.

If the number you get from this calculation is less than 18.5, the child is considered underweight; between 18.5 and 25 is considered normal healthy weight; a number between 25 to 30 is considered overweight; and a number more than 30 is considered obese.

Hydration: Fuel for Activities

Water is essential for good health. Did you know that water makes up about 60 percent of a child's body weight? Every cell, tissue, and organ needs water to function correctly. Getting enough fluids is important to staying healthy. Also, water tends to help preschool children do better in school. A dehydrated preschooler may have as much as a 20 percent reduction in physical and mental performance.

Water helps children when they are physically active. Except for oxygen, there is nothing a child's body needs more than an ample supply of water. The more active a child is, the more he needs to drink the right amount of water before, during, and after physical activity. If a child is well hydrated, then his heart does not have to work as hard to pump blood to his body, and his muscles will work more efficiently. If a child complains of being thirsty or wants to continually sit and rest, it may be because he is dehydrated.

Fluids—especially water—play an important role in making sure children are hydrated. Children lose some body water every day in the form of sweat, tears, and going to the bathroom. Water also leaves the body when a child breathes. Larger amounts of water are lost during vigorous physical activity.

Encouraging Physical Activity in Preschoolers

The best way to prevent dehydration is to make sure children get plenty of fluids when they are physically active. They should consume more fluids than they lose. It is especially important that children drink often during hot weather. Those who participate in sports or strenuous activities should drink some extra fluid before the activity begins, should drink at regular intervals (about every twenty minutes) during the course of the activity, and should drink after it ends. Ideally, physical activity should be scheduled for the early morning or late afternoon to avoid the hottest part of the day.

Thirst is not a reliable early sign of dehydration. By the time a child feels thirsty, he may already be dehydrated. Sometimes, thirst can be quenched before the necessary body fluids have been replaced. That is why children should start drinking before thirst develops and should consume additional fluids even after thirst is quenched.

A child who is mildly dehydrated from overexertion will probably be thirsty and should be allowed to drink as much as he wants. Plain water is the best option. Also, the child should rest in a cool, shaded environment until the lost fluid has been replaced.

Preschoolers are at greater risk of becoming dehydrated than adults, in part because they are less effective at perspiring and because their bodies can produce more heat during exercise. If you have ever watched children play, you know that they get so wrapped up in what they are doing that they often forget to break for a drink. That is why it is so important for adults to help them stay hydrated.

Even though a child's body may be smaller than yours, he still needs lots of water. The American Academy of Pediatrics recommends that children drink six glasses of water on an average day. Recommendations for preschool children include about five additional ounces (or two child-size gulps) of water every twenty minutes during vigorous physical activity.

Water is the best form of liquid for children. Soda is not good because of the phosphate and sugar and because it may cause children to lose more fluid and become dehydrated quicker. When a child is dehydrated, his internal temperature goes up. For a child's body to function properly during play, it must be hydrated. Most experts agree that children need about ½ cup of water per hour. When it is hot outside, more water may be needed. Take steps to help children get the most out of play time:

- Remind them to drink water throughout the day, even when they are not feeling thirsty.
- Keep a water bottle handy when they are playing outside.
- Provide foods filled with water, such as grapes or watermelon.
- Water down their juice—half juice, half water—to provide more hydration and less sugar.
- Cut out all sodas.
- Call for regular water breaks during play time.
- Remind them to drink before and after prolonged physical activity.
- Be a good role model and drink water throughout the day. Children are likely to follow your lead.
- Drink water when you go to a restaurant. Not only does it keep children hydrated, but it is usually free!

Encouraging Physical Activity in Preschoolers

Kicking the Soda Habit

Drinking soda has become a habit for many people in the United States. Calories from sugar-sweetened beverages in the form of sugar or high fructose corn syrup are taking over the diets of our children. Most sodas provide no nutritional value and add unneeded calories. Many researchers point to soda, along with a lack of physical activity, as a leading cause of childhood obesity. For the health of children, it is time to remove soda from their diets and add the most readily available alternative—water.

Sugar in the form of soda is sometimes referred to as "liquid candy" by health officials. Children who drink soda do not feel as full as if they had eaten the same calories from solid food and typically eat more than they normally would. The average can of sugar-sweetened soda provides about 150 calories. If a child were to drink just 12 ounces of a sugar-sweetened soft drink every day and not cut back on calories elsewhere, she would gain 5 pounds more than she normally would each year. Strong evidence also indicates that sugar-sweetened soft drinks contribute to the development of diabetes.

A child needs a healthy body to participate daily in physical activity. In addition to causing weight gain and increasing the chances of diabetes, soft drinks and too much sugar also can have an impact on healthy bones. Calcium is important to normal bone growth and is not found in soft drinks, although phosphate is. Consuming more phosphate than calcium can affect normal bone growth. Researchers have found that children who

SODA— DID YOU KNOW?

A can of soda contains about 150 calories. One 12-ounce soda would make up about 10 percent of the calories a child needs each day. Just imagine if a child had three or four sodas each day and consumed 30-40 percent of her daily needed calories from soda? If a child consumed this much soda, it would be easy to understand why she would be gaining unnecessary weight. A typical ten-year-old has to bike vigorously for thirty minutes to burn the calories in a 12-ounce soda. Health officials estimate that most U.S. children are getting about 15 teaspoons of refined sugar daily from sweetened beverages. This is more sugar than children should be getting from all foods in any day's time.

consume more soft drinks consume less milk and receive less calcium for growing bones.

Experts recommend limiting or eliminating sweetened beverages from children's diets. Replace sugar-loaded drinks with water, unsweetened beverages, and low-fat or nonfat milk. This step is an important part of encouraging children to be healthy and physically active.

Best
Strategies
for Learning
Physical Skills

Children can get only so far in the development of essential physical skills without some guidance from a knowledgeable adult. As pediatrician Benjamin Spock noted in *The Pocket Book of Baby and Child Care,* children supply the power, but they need adults to steer them. In other words, children bring the enthusiasm and energy to learn, and caring adults supply guidance at the appropriate time.

Your guidance is crucial as children strive to learn to kick a ball, ride a bike, or jump rope. You do not need any special physical skills to teach children to throw or strike a ball; you just need to learn effective strategies for supporting children's physical development. The first steps are simply to choose to participate and create time each day for physical activities.

A common misconception is that young children just naturally learn how to kick, throw, catch, and strike. Some children will develop physical skills without assistance from adults, but the majority will not. Time to practice skills should be scheduled daily. It is essential for caregivers and parents to be involved in the skill-development process. A survey of people in the United States who participate regularly in outdoor physical activity found that 90 percent of them began doing so between the ages of five and eighteen.

Stand Back and Watch

Getting started is easy! Any time you want to help children learn new physical skills, let them lead the way. In line with educator Maria Montessori's philosophy, help children try activities on their own. Never begin by providing instruction. The preschool years are a time for children to explore, experiment, and solve challenges on their own. Do not get in the way; your initial role is to have the patience to step back and observe children playing with balls, climbing on the playground equipment, or running across the playground.

Honestly, it is not easy to just stand back and limit your involvement. Sometimes caregivers and parents have a tendency to want to help children too much. The first step in introducing a new skill is to place children in the appropriate environment and provide the equipment needed—then step back and simply let them play. For example, if you want children to learn how to kick a ball, take them to the playground or backyard. Provide a soft, lightweight ball, and simply ask the child to kick it. She may pick the ball up and throw it into the air or try to bounce it. Eventually she will get around to kicking. It is great for you to play with her. Kick the ball to the child, and ask that she kick it back. But, this is not the time for instruction—it is the child's time to explore what she can do with the ball and play with you.

It is your time to observe and get an understanding of the child's initial skills. Later, you will be able to tell when the child is ready for skill instruction.

The preschool years are the ideal time for children to develop a foundation of the physical skills they will use and refine throughout their lives. Most three-year-olds are in a precontrol or initial stage of skill development. They will attempt to gallop, skip, throw, catch, and kick, but their movements are simple and uncoordinated. A child in this stage may be unable to repeat movements in succession, and one attempt at a skill does not look like another attempt to perform the same movement.

By ages four and five, most children have progressed to a controlled stage in which movements are less haphazard and seem to conform more to the child's intentions. Movements will appear more consistent, and repetitions are somewhat alike. By age eight most children have the developmental potential to reach a more mature stage in most of the basic physical skills. Movements will be more automatic and can be performed successfully with concentration. By this age, a child should be able to use an individual skill in combination with other skills. For example, she can catch a ball and then throw it in a game situation or can dribble a ball while running down the court.

Even though all children go through similar developmental stages, we cannot assume that they will develop physical skills simply because they get older. Many children will develop locomotor or traveling skills (walking, running, galloping) on their own. Children naturally practice and improve those skills as long as they have opportunities to do so. However, some physical skills require adult assistance for the child to achieve a more mature form of the skill. In that case, your role is to guide them with instruction and to encourage repeated practice.

What makes this process so interesting is that children are growing and maturing in other areas also. By age three, children are becoming less dependent on caregivers and more dependent on themselves. Preschoolers begin to cooperate with others during play and are forming friendships with other children. They can regulate their emotions, and behavior improves greatly. Children are eager to please their caregivers and parents, but they are increasingly in the time of life where they want to do everything themselves.

Encouraging Physical Activity in Preschoolers

Adult-Initiated Activities

Many preschool teachers believe that children learn best when they can explore, manipulate materials, and acquire skills through their own experiences. Along with child-guided explorations, a fair amount of caregiver- or parent-guided experiences also are needed when children are learning physical skills. At some point, you will have the opportunity to present information to the children, model skills, and guide the learning process. Ideally, you should strive for balance between exploration by the children and learning activities guided by adults, as preschool teachers do when leading other classroom activities.

Learning about physical activity is not a completely independent adventure for children. Adults must be involved. After providing ample time (sometimes weeks or months, depending on the skill) for initial play and exploration, you will need to share specific information and allow time for practice. Your job will be to find appropriate tasks and the appropriate degree of difficulty to match the developmental level of the child.

Providing Appropriate Tasks

Tasks simply provide a child with direction on practicing a skill. For example, consider some appropriate beginning tasks: "Throw the ball and hit the target." "See how far you can kick the ball." "Can you jump off both feet at the same time and land on both feet?" As you design tasks to help children improve their motor skills, make sure you present the tasks with a definite purpose and logical progression. In addition, present activities so that children will have high rates of success. Keep the tasks simple, but give children enough direction so they know how to practice a specific skill. The activity sections of this book contain sample tasks to get you started.

Improving skill takes lots of practice. We know from research that children who practice skills at a high rate of success are more likely to continue practicing and thus have more opportunities to improve. Children who are given tasks that are too hard tend to get frustrated and soon stop practicing. Children who are given tasks that are too easy tend to get bored and soon stop practicing. Research suggests that the most appropriate success rate for children to practice a physical skill is 70 to 80 percent.

You can test this idea of high success rates. Set up a target outside on a wall or tree. Make sure the target is at least 12 inches by 12 inches and is placed at the shoulder height of the child (36 to 48 inches off the ground). Place a mark on the ground 2 feet from the target, and ask the child to stand behind the mark and throw ten times. Record how many times the child hits the target. Now place a mark on the ground 30 feet from the target, and again ask the child to throw ten times at the target from behind the mark. Most preschool children will hit the target ten out of ten times at the first distance, but most will be able to hit the target only two or three times from the far distance, if at all. At the short distance, the child will quickly get bored with the activity; at the far distance, he will soon become frustrated with his lack of success.

Your next step is to find a distance from the target where the child can consistently throw and strike the target seven or eight times out of ten. This is where children will feel the most success and get the most practice without getting bored or frustrated. Each child will have a different distance from the target that works best. When you create tasks with the optimum success rate, you will encourage more practice and will make improved development more likely. Children who are frustrated or bored during practice get turned off to physical activity and are less likely to develop a mature form of the basic physical skills.

Refining the Skill

The next step in a child's efforts to learn physical skills depends on you. After practicing the tasks you have provided, the child will be ready for input on how to perform the skill better. You may be wondering how to take it to the next level: "What can I say to a child to help her jump off both feet and land without falling over?" "What can I say to a child to help her throw a ball better?"

Refining the skill requires that we look at the mechanics of how the mature form of the skill is performed. For example, the most efficient, skillful way to throw a ball is to step forward on the opposite foot from the throwing arm before releasing the ball. If the child is right-handed, she would step

Learning a new skill takes a long time. Children do not necessarily learn fundamental movement skills naturally as part of their normal growth and development. Research on skill development suggests that it may take up to 600 minutes of instruction over a period of several years for children to learn different motor skills. If you underestimate the amount of time it takes to master these skills and teach too much too soon, you and the child may get frustrated.

forward on the left foot when throwing; the left-handed child steps forward on the right foot. Stepping on the same foot as the hand that holds the ball places the body off balance and makes it more difficult to accurately throw the ball.

The most mechanically sound way to walk across a balance beam is to hold the arms straight out from the sides of the body. This helps the body stay on balance as the child moves across the beam. The most mechanically sound way to jump over something is to swing the arms from back to front when jumping. These are examples of *skill refinements* or *cues*. Cues are teaching points that provide children with specific steps that help them learn a skill quickly and correctly. The appropriate cue also may keep children from forming bad habits. Telling a preschool child to "keep your eye on the ball (keep looking at it)" when she is attempting to catch would be an appropriate cue. Similarly, saying, "Swing your arms when you jump," will help the child better understand the mechanics of jumping.

All physical skills have several refinements that can be helpful in learning the skill. For example, in learning to throw, there are four important basic cues:

- Hold the throwing arm way back.
- Keep your side to the target.
- Step with the opposite foot.
- Follow through.

This sounds like a lot to learn, which is why you should not overload children with all the cues for a specific skill at once. Cues should be introduced and practiced over a period of several years, if necessary. The rule for presenting cues to children is that you discuss one cue at a time. When the child has begun to understand one cue, then another can be introduced.

The activity section of this book contains suggested teaching points or cues for you to use with preschool children. Selected cues have also been included here as a quick reference.

Cues for Practicing Traveling Skills

- Walking—swing arms, keep head up, stay on balance when stopping
- Running—swing arms, bend elbows, head up, balanced stops
- Skipping—lift knees high, hop and land on one foot, hop and land on the other
- Galloping—take a big step and lead with that foot

Cues for Practicing Balance Skills

- Jumping and landing—bend knees, swing arms, land on both feet at the same time, balance without falling
- Balancing—maintain stillness, keep center of gravity (point where body's weight is concentrated) over base of support, extend arms

Cues for Practicing Manipulative Skills

- Throwing—side to the target, hold arm way back, step with opposite foot, follow through
- Catching—watch the ball, reach, pull ball into body
- Kicking—contact ball with instep or shoelaces, nonkicking foot beside ball, watch the ball
- Volleying—contact ball with a flat body surface, get body ready, watch ball, and move body to get ready
- Dribbling—use fingers, hands on top of ball
- Striking—keep eye on ball, level swing, hold paddle or bat way back, follow through

Promoting Continual Practice

Even for children, fun activities sometimes become uninteresting. They may get tired of an activity and no longer want to practice. However, regular practice of skills should continue throughout the preschool years. Two strategies to keep children practicing and improving are repetition and timing.

Repetitions encourage children to meet suggested goals. "Can you jump over the rope and land without falling five times in a row?" "Can you jump rope twenty times without stopping?" "Can you kick a ball in the goal from 10 feet away seven out of ten times?" Keep in mind that a task is more challenging if the activity is measurable. You may even want to further motivate the child by posting the tasks on a chart. Record his efforts, and praise him for achieving the goals. "Today you were able to strike the punch ball in the air with your hands twenty-five times in a row. The next time we practice striking, maybe you can try thirty times in a row."

You also can provide a challenge and motivate the child to keep practicing by adding timing to the task. Timing is a self-testing technique that allows children to compete against the clock. You can use the following types of prompts:

- "Can you hop for ten seconds without touching both feet to the floor?"
- "Can you skip to the tree and back before I count to fifteen?"
- "Can you stand on one foot for twelve seconds without moving?"

As you work with children to develop physical skills, you will find lots of opportunities to add repetition and timing activities. These challenges encourage children to keep practicing skills. Remember that a challenge does not change the activity or task; it simply makes it measurable and helps to further motivate the child to practice.

Modeling Physical Skills

Part of helping children develop physical skills is your participation. Do not stand back and watch all the time; at some point you may need to demonstrate how to do a skill. This demonstration is called *modeling* and is used to show a child how to do an activity or task. It does not matter if you are talented at performing the skill or if you are awkward and clumsy—the child does not care. Many children learn better when they can see how a physical skill can be done. Your job is to model how to do the activity when needed.

Some children may not need your modeling, yet others will depend on it—they learn best by first seeing how the skill is to be performed. Even if you are not good at the skill, you can demonstrate parts of it. If you are practicing throwing, you may not be accurate at it, but you can demonstrate that you step with the opposite foot. You may not be the best at jumping rope, but you can demonstrate the correct way for children to hold the rope. You should model skills whenever children need visual guidance.

Another method of modeling is to ask the child to watch an older friend or sibling do the skill. Some children may understand better if they see a peer do the skill instead of an adult. If you use this method, make sure the child demonstrating is doing the skill correctly. For example, "Watch Danielle. See how she holds her arms straight out from her sides to help stay balanced when walking on the beam?" Children should not try to copy a movement exactly, but they can observe others and get ideas. Some children will pick up the skill better from watching adults, and others will learn more quickly from watching their peers.

Providing Feedback

Tasks, cues, and challenges—along with modeling—are important ways of presenting information to children. However, the most crucial strategy you can use to promote successful skill development is providing appropriate feedback. Your comments let the children know that you are watching and that physical skill development is important. Without feedback, a child may practice a skill incorrectly and have to correct a bad habit later. Encourage the children to continue to practice, and let them know if they are doing the skill correctly. They really cannot determine their level of success on their own.

Your approval is important to inspire children to practice and learn new skills. Giving general feedback about a skill—making comments such as "Good job," "Terrific," "I like the way you throw," or "You are really good at jumping"—helps demonstrate that you approve of what the children are doing and encourages them to continue practicing. However, general feedback does not provide children with information on how to improve their skills. They stop listening if all they hear is, "Excellent," when they know they have done the task poorly.

Use specific feedback often. Your guidance is specific when it contains information that allows children to know exactly what they need to practice to get better at a skill. Comments usually include information about the skill refinement or cue. If adults give feedback about how to do the skill better, children can adjust their actions for more success. Using specific feedback, however, does not mean you cannot give general feedback as well. The two types can work together to encourage children to practice and improve skills. Here are some examples of using specific and general feedback together:

- "Terrific. I like the way you stepped with your opposite foot."
- "Nice job holding your arms out to the side."
- "Good job swinging your arms when you jump."
- "It's great to see you using your fingertips to dribble the ball."

POSITIVE AND NEGATIVE FEEDBACK

When children feel frustrated because they cannot do a skill well or do it perfectly the first time, try to discourage them from feeling and talking negatively about themselves. Encourage children to give themselves positive feedback, such as the following types of statements:

- "I am great at running."
- "I really like throwing the ball because I can throw far."
- "I can do it."

Positive self-talk will help children build confidence in their abilities and will encourage the desire to be physically active and improve on physical skills.

Keep in mind that feedback can be positive or negative. Positive feedback is always best. By encouraging children, you are creating a pleasant environment where learning can take place. If children feel as if they are always doing something wrong, they may get turned off to practicing. Negative feedback can affect how the child feels about his ability to do a skill. So be sensitive and strive to provide positive feedback. Adults providing instruction should commit to verbally reinforcing children's successes and to using specific and positive feedback to help them understand how skills could be done better. Children thrive on positive feedback; it will help them gain confidence that they can learn new skills. The following examples show positive feedback specific to skill development:

- "I like the way you are holding the racket."
- "I could really see how much you were trying when you kicked the ball with the inside of your foot."
- "I'm so proud that you were able to hit the target eight out of ten times."
- "You really showed your skill when you were able to bounce the ball with your fingertips and dribble around the cones."
- "Congratulations on walking across the beam with your arms out to the side."
- "What an imagination! You have thought of five ways to balance on different body parts."
- "You are so clever to use that basket for a target."
- "I knew you could swing the bat and hit the ball. Keeping your eye on the ball really helps."

Further Encouragement

In addition to working with children one-on-one, you can encourage them by being an active role model and having a positive attitude about physical activity. If the children see you enjoying physical activity and having fun, it can encourage them to participate. Good habits are best started early.

Caregivers can encourage physical activity by taking children on walks or dancing to music with them, for example. Parents can encourage activity

by playing with children in the backyard, taking the family to the park, or going on a bike ride together. Help the children play and move around by purchasing equipment such as balls, bats, paddles, and jump ropes. Limit the amount of time preschoolers spend watching television or playing computer games to no more than two hours per day. Provide a good example for children in the following ways:

- Regularly participate in physical activity yourself.
- Talk with the children about the activities you find enjoyable or compete in.
- Allow children to choose the types of activities they are interested in.
- Help children develop skills and strategies for coping with different environments for physical activity.
- Involve children in activities around the home or center that require active movement such as gardening, washing the car, or cleaning.

- Encourage and support walking and biking; you can even walk instead of taking the car for nearby errands or visits.
- Spend time at the park or pool, hike in the woods, or participate in dance classes.

As children strive to develop and refine physical skills, they want and need your participation. They want to know how they are doing, and they particularly want your input on how to improve and do a skill better. Let the fun begin!

Physical
Activity
Environment

Inspiring children to be active requires space and appropriate equipment; therefore, the physical environment influences children's skill development. Creating a setting and atmosphere that will encourage exploration and physical development is important for children of all ages. Keep in mind that you can influence the lifelong health of children by ensuring that the environment where they spend time has appropriate equipment and storage areas, an adult role model, and a safe space for daily activity.

The physical activity environment for preschoolers needs to be carefully and thoughtfully organized. This does not mean that the environment should always be neat or that activities should be overly structured, but the environment should be functional. The environment you create for play and practice communicates a message to children about the importance of physical activity. Find a large, outdoor, open space that is safe, and make sure you have plenty of the appropriate skill-development equipment and a place to store it. When you have taken care of these things, it is time to take the most important step—go play together and have fun!

Preschool Environment

About 50 percent of three- and four-year-old children in the United States attend some type of preschool program outside of the home. The physical-activity environment at preschool should follow developmentally appropriate guidelines and should include indoor and outdoor spaces for movement, a curriculum and progression of activities, daily scheduled activity classes, and enough appropriate equipment so that every child

can participate in an activity without waiting in line for a turn. Preschools should provide some type of physical-skill assessment similar to assessments for academic skills. The environment should also include activities that promote success and provide for repetition of activities that encourage skill development. Parents trying to decide on a preschool for their children should understand that all physical-activity programs at preschools are not the same. Ask about the physical-activity program before making a decision about a preschool. Are skill development and play scheduled daily? Is there enough equipment to prevent waiting in lines to play? Have teachers been trained to help children learn basic physical skills?

SCHOOL MOVEMENT PROGRAMS FOR PRESCHOOL CHILDREN— DID YOU KNOW?

In the past many child care facilities and preschools did not have physical education programs for preschool children, but this practice has changed. Shape America recommends that quality, daily physical-activity experiences be available for all children at school and home. Physical-activity classes should focus on learning basic motor skills. The school environment should include activities, equipment, and instruction necessary to maximize opportunities to be successful in learning fundamental skills.

Preschool Playgroups

Creating a comfortable and safe physical-activity environment and playing together are great ways to help children begin to develop and refine physical skills. You also will want to organize times when children can practice skills with peers. Forming a preschool playgroup is an excellent way to promote physical activity among children in home-based care environments. A playgroup should consist of children of a similar age and two or more adults. The group could meet weekly in someone's backyard or at a local park. Set a day, time, and place to meet regularly. Be sure to pack water so everyone remains hydrated during the activities.

A playgroup will give children opportunities to socialize and make friends while developing their physical skills. Remember that there will be balls flying everywhere. You do not need a lot of rules, but make sure that all children understand the safety rules required—for example, do not get too close to each other when swinging a racket or kicking a ball. Children will learn by observing each other. Furthermore, some caregivers and parents feel uncomfortable demonstrating a skill to children because they cannot do it well. In those situations, they can call on other adults to assist.

Schedule about an hour, and bring a mesh bag full of equipment. Let children explore and experiment with equipment items, but select a focus each time you meet. You can concentrate on kicking activities one week and on throwing activities the next. Have the entire group help put away equipment when play time is over. It is never too early to introduce children to expectations of cooperation with others during physical activity. Having

children do activities together—such as getting out and putting away equipment, throwing balls at the same target, walking across a log in the woods, or climbing a playground structure—will help them develop skills that can lead to positive sportsmanship and enjoyment of cooperative and competitive physical activities in the future.

Taking It Outside

Playing outside on the playground or in the backyard is a natural pastime for most children. It is important to provide plenty of space for running, jumping, throwing, kicking, and striking. Because this space does not exist inside most homes and few preschools have large indoor gym spaces, preschoolers need to be outdoors for these activities. Outdoor space can be found at a local park, at a sports field, in the backyard, or across the street in the yard of a neighbor. Most schools have large grassy spaces for outdoor play. This area should be free from safety hazards (such as glass, debris, and water), located away from buildings or playground structures, and have clearly defined physical boundaries. Create a safety zone where children can play, by marking corners of the open zone with cones or small

Encouraging Physical Activity in Preschoolers

There are no published guidelines for the amount of space appropriate for physical activity in the backyard. But if you apply guidance used in school physical-activity settings, you should have at least 150 square feet of open space per child to safely practice skill-development activities. So a school playground or backyard with about 10 feet by 15 feet of space to move freely is the minimum needed.

markers on the ground. Remove all obstacles that might hinder a child's movement and be a safety concern. Even if you are restricted to a relatively small space, you can move large objects to the corner of the play area.

The term *sedentary* suggests that someone is sitting most of the time and getting little exercise. We do not want children to be sedentary, yet many parents and preschools provide an environment filled with activities that do not give children the opportunity to move. Sitting while watching TV and playing video games has become part of the culture for preschoolers. Some caregivers and teachers allow children to sit out of physical activities instead of encouraging participation. Research from the Nielsen Company suggests that, on average, children ages two to five spent about thirty-two hours a week in front of a TV in 2009. If we really want to reduce childhood obesity and provide an environment that encourages physical activity, we should simply turn off the TV. Almost anything else children can do uses more energy than watching TV.

Moving to the Music

Whether preschool children are indoors or out, have you ever watched what happens when music is playing? They move! Music and physical activity naturally go together. You can encourage movement by including a variety of music in the background when children are playing. Some experts suggest that moving to music can be an effective tool for learning and might be as important as learning the alphabet, numbers, or how to kick or throw a ball.

Research suggests that children who are actively involved with music (playing it, singing it, or listening to it regularly) do better in reading and math when they start school, are better able to focus and control their bodies, play better with others, and have higher self-esteem. Moving to music helps a young child learn about his body parts and have an understanding of moving to a rhythmical pattern. This understanding may help him know when to swing a bat so it will strike a ball, coordinate when

to swing his leg forward to kick, or synchronize how to move his body parts smoothly when galloping or skipping. Music helps children develop a sense of patterning during movement activities. Encourage children to listen to music at home and to sing and move along.

Skill-Development Equipment

Each part of a child's education requires appropriate learning materials. For example, if children are learning how to read and write, they might need pencils, crayons, paper, alphabet puzzles, and books. Children learning about math might need counting blocks, geometric shapes, and number puzzles.

Children also need appropriate materials and equipment to learn about physical skills. To learn how to throw, children need different sizes and shapes of balls. To develop skill in striking, children need rackets or bats. Children cannot learn how to jump rope without a rope. When children are learning how to kick, they need balls.

As you make selections, be careful to match the equipment with the age and skill level of the child. For example, a baseball would definitely not be suitable for teaching a four-year-old to throw and catch. A full-sized adult football would be inappropriate for developing punting skills. Using an adult-sized golf club to teach striking skills could be disastrous. In each case, the equipment

item mentioned is too dangerous, too heavy, or the wrong size for a child trying to develop basic skills.

So you are probably wondering what equipment is needed and where you can find it. You may also be wondering what equipment you can make yourself. The next section describes the types of equipment you will need to get started and provides directions on how to build items that you cannot easily find in stores. Most equipment for developing basic skills can be found in toy or sport retail stores. Teachers at preschools will have access to physical-education equipment catalogs that stock a variety of appropriate items. Although you can purchase lots of equipment and spend lots of money, you will be amazed at how short this starter equipment list really is and at the relatively low expense involved. Remember that for full participation, you need enough appropriate equipment for all children. If you have ten children kicking balls, throwing beanbags, or jumping rope, then each child will need a ball, beanbag, or jump rope to be successful developing skills.

Balance Beams

Balance beams give children a chance to practice balance skills by moving on a narrow strip of wood usually 4 to 6 inches wide. Purchased beams can be expensive. You can make a balance beam using a 4" x 4" piece of wood that is 6 to 8 feet long. Sand the beam to remove rough spots and splinters. Have the child help select a paint color and paint the beam. Place a base on each end to raise the beam an additional 2 inches above the ground. The base stabilizes the beam as children move back and forth. You do not necessarily need a balance beam at home; instead, you can use a log in the woods, the curb along a low-traffic street, or a balance beam on a playground.

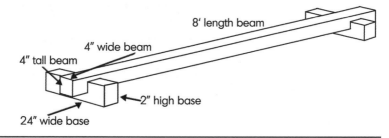

8' length beam

4" wide beam

4" tall beam

2" high base

24" wide base

Dimensions for constructing your own balance beam.

Balls

Obtain lightweight foam, rubber, and plastic balls; old tennis balls; whiffle balls; and beach balls. Have a variety available in different sizes, but make sure they are no larger than 10 inches in diameter. Look for bright colors that are easy for a child to track.

Punch-Ball Balloons

The best balloon to use is called a punch-ball balloon, which can be found in most toy stores. Punch balls are durable and move slowly through the air, so children have a better opportunity to learn to throw, catch, and strike. Smaller balloons are not as thick and durable. Blow up the punch ball to about 16 inches in diameter. **Safety caution:** Never let a small child blow up any balloon because it can be a choking hazard! If a balloon pops, immediately pick up the pieces and throw them away.

INCLUDING ALL CHILDREN

Some children may have an allergic reaction to latex. An inflated beach ball could be substituted for the punch ball.

Balance Boards

A balance board is easy to make and offers a fun way to practice and develop static balancing skill. When using the board, the child is placed in off-balance positions and then given time to distribute her weight over the middle axis of the board to achieve balance. Balance boards are designed to be challenging but not frustrating.

If you would like to construct your own balance board, you can use ½-inch thick plywood cut 10 inches wide and 15 inches long. On the bottom attach an 8-inch-long section of 2" x 2", 2" x 3", or 2" x 4" lumber to the center of the board. Use screws (from top) and glue to attach. Any lumber will work, but birch plywood is most durable.

A board with a 4-inch-high center piece can be used as the child advances in skill, but the 2- and 3-inch-high boards should be used for the center in the beginning. After constructing the boards, you can initiate an art project and have the children help sand the rough edges and paint the board.

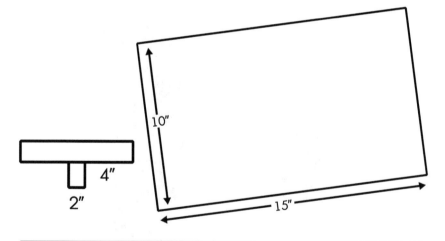

Dimensions for constructing your own balance board.

Bats, Hockey Sticks, and Golf Clubs

Plastic bats work better than wooden bats when introducing striking skills. Wooden bats are too heavy for most preschool children. Plastic bats are lighter, safer, and easier for young children to swing. Bats are usually about 28 inches long and 3 to 4 inches in diameter. Another option is to use plastic or foam hockey sticks. Foam sticks are made out of Ethafoam material and are very safe; they can also be used to practice the golf swing.

Beanbags

Square and cubed beanbags are great for throwing and catching. Square beanbags are usually 4 or 5 inches on each side and filled with plastic pellets. Cubed beanbags may be easier to catch because they better fit a child's hands. The cubed beanbag can be made by cutting material into two 2" x 6" rectangles and sewing the material together to form a cube. Before sewing the final end closed, fill the cube with plastic pellets. Bright colors work well for beanbags.

Cones

Traffic cones are used as boundary markers; they can also serve as tees when children are striking balls with paddles and bats.

Hoops

Hoops usually come in 24-, 30-, and 36-inch diameters and are made of plastic. Smaller diameters may work best for younger children.

Jump Ropes

The best type of jump rope to use with young children is one 7 feet long with plastic beads along the length to add extra weight to help children swing the rope over their heads. A longer rope tends to tangle; a shorter rope is more difficult for children to get over their heads.

Jump Box

Jump boxes can be purchased, or you can construct one from ¾-inch plywood. Cut carrying holes in two opposite sides of the box. Make sure all rough edges are sanded. If you like, you can get children to help paint and decorate it. On the side of the box, you can tape photos or clippings of children and adults jumping. You can make the box fancy by attaching a piece of carpet on top for the take-off area. Using ¾-inch plywood will make the box heavy enough that it will not move when children jump off. The box can also be used as an equipment storage container.

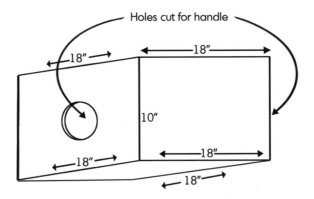

Holes cut for handle

18" 18" 10" 18" 18"

Construct a jump box that is 18 inches wide and 10 inches tall on each side, with a top that is square and 18 inches on each side.

Launch Board

A launch board propels a ball or beanbag into the air directly in front of the child, and thus she does not need to be skilled at tossing the ball into the air. Launch boards are easy to make. Use ¼-inch-thick birch plywood, 30 inches long and 5 inches wide. Seven inches from one end, attach a 5-inch-long, 1½-inch-diameter dowel stick with glue and screws. If you are using a ball, cut a 2-inch-diameter hole in the end of the board to place the ball. A cubed beanbag works well because it easily fits into a child's small hands.

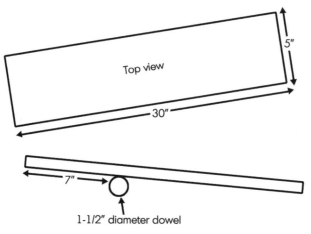

You can construct your own launch board using these dimensions.

Paddles and Rackets

Paddles are made of foam, plastic, or wood and have a handle. If children will be striking punch-ball balloons, a Ping-Pong paddle works well. There are different lengths of handles on paddles. Have children start out using shorter handles, and save the longer handles for when they have developed higher skill levels. Try to find rackets that are lightweight, as a heavier paddle will hinder the child's swing.

Scarves

Scarves can be thrown, caught, and used in rhythm activities. Lightweight, silk-like scarves fall slowly when tossed, so they will be easier for the child to catch. Scarves for young children are usually 12 to 16 inches square.

Target Boards

There are lots of different things that can be used to make a target. Make a box or circle shape on an outside wall using bright-colored tape. You can also paint or draw a target on a paper plate or large sheet of paper or cardboard, then tape it on a wall or attach it to a large tree. You can purchase targets or construct your own.

Wooden targets can be constructed from ¾-inch-thick plywood. Cut a 32-inch square for the target surface, and cut different-shaped holes in the board—circle, square, triangle, and rectangle. Supports are constructed so that the target leans back slightly and so that the bottoms of the supports are wider than the tops. This allows the target to be used for both overhand and underhand throws. Attach supports to the target with nails and glue.

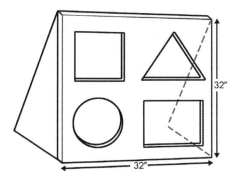

32″
32″
3/4″ plywood

Scoops

Plastic scoops serve as extensions of children's hands and arms to help develop their catching skills. Homemade scoops can be made from plastic milk jugs. A scoop can really be an advantage if a child is having difficulty catching or has special needs.

Tidy Equipment Storage

Children may not always stop moving to put away their playthings, which can make the home or school environment look like an obstacle course. Make sure you have a designated spot for physical-activity equipment. Without a storage plan, you will spend time tripping over equipment and looking for lost items that later turn up under a piece of furniture or outside in the rain. It should be the children's responsibility to get equipment out and put equipment away. You should take the responsibility of figuring out where it should be stored.

A few strategies will make it easier for children to clean up after play. You will get a space free of clutter, and the children will learn some valuable skills about putting things away after use. The following simple ideas will help with equipment storage:

● Decide on a place for storage somewhere close to the door where equipment can be gathered, or set up storage everywhere equipment

Encouraging Physical Activity in Preschoolers

tends to land. You may decide to have two or three equipment locations in your center or home.

- It is important that equipment storage be child accessible. Make use of hooks, plastic storage bins or boxes, and open shelves that are sturdy enough for constant use.
- So there is no question about what goes where, label everything. To help young children, attach photos to shelves and bins with clear packing tape.
- Equipment should be easy to get to and move. You may want to consider a small cart with wheels that can be rolled outside. Certainly mesh bags will be helpful for equipment when transporting several items to the park or backyard.

Safety Guidelines

Preschoolers need many opportunities to practice new skills, so be sure to provide a variety of appropriate, safe equipment in good working order. Keep children safe without being overprotective. The activity environment must provide safe space without obstacles or dangerous playground equipment. Consider safety anywhere you take children to play. Having a safe environment will help you to challenge children to develop physical skills and not turn them off to physical activity because of a bad experience related to an injury. Whether children are playing on the playground or in the backyard, follow these guidelines to ensure safety:

- Check equipment each time children play to be sure nothing is broken. It is a good idea to check when you are gathering equipment to go outside.
- Continually check the activity space and any playground equipment for such things as exposed nails and broken parts.
- Do not lift children onto play equipment that they cannot climb onto by themselves. Swings are an exception to this general rule.
- Watch out for high places—such as slides and monkey bars—that can be dangerous to young children. Falling from high places is the most frequent cause of serious injuries on the playground.

- Allow children to experiment with mild risks that build feelings of competence as challenges are met and mastered, but do not place children at risk simply as a challenge to see if they can accomplish a task.

- Families do not need to have play sets in the backyard, but children should be climbing at least three to four times each week. You can take them to the local park to climb.

- Supervision is a must on the playground or in the backyard, but it is especially critical when children are on a play structure. Make sure there is always a padded landing (soft, deep surfaces such as sand or bark mulch beneath high equipment), and teach children the best way to land. Whenever possible, they should land on both feet. Grass is not soft enough to adequately cushion a fall.

Encouraging Physical Activity in Preschoolers

ACCIDENTS— DID YOU KNOW?

Safety in the gym, on the playground, or in the backyard should be a top concern. A study from the U.S. Consumer Product Safety Commission found that from 2001 to 2008 more than 200,000 children visited emergency rooms each year for playground-related accidents.

The U.S. Consumer Product Safety Commission provides a checklist to help make sure your local community or school playground is a safe place to play:

- Ensure that surfaces around playground equipment consist of least 12 inches of wood chips, mulch, sand, or pea gravel; or use mats made of safety-tested rubber or rubber-like materials.
- Extend protective surfacing at least 6 feet in all directions from the play equipment. For swings, surfacing should extend, in back and front, to twice the height of the suspending bar.
- For play structures more than 30 inches high, make sure they are spaced at least 9 feet apart.

- Check to be sure that the equipment does not have dangerous hardware, such as open *S* hooks or protruding bolt ends.
- If the equipment has spaces that could potentially trap children, such as openings in guardrails or between ladder rungs, they should measure less than 3.5 inches or more than 9 inches.
- Make sure the equipment does not have sharp points or edges.
- Avoid tripping hazards, such as exposed concrete footings, tree stumps, and rocks.
- Ensure that elevated surfaces, such as platforms and ramps, have guardrails to prevent falls.
- Check playgrounds regularly to verify that equipment and protective surfaces are in good condition.
- Carefully supervise children on playgrounds to keep them safe.

Creating a child-friendly activity area for your center or home takes a bit of planning, but the time and effort put toward creating safe, easy-to-care-for play areas will be well worth it. The benefits of having a yard designed with children in mind will be readily apparent as you watch them enjoy the space. Meanwhile, you will enjoy the advantages of convenient cleanup and the need for fewer bandages for cuts and scrapes.

Encouraging Physical Activity in Preschoolers

You may wonder what else you can do to help your child be active. Consider these ideas:

- Be an active role model and have a positive attitude. If children watch you enjoying physical activity, it can foster their participation.

- Urge children to play actively on the playground or in the backyard, go for a fast walk, dance to music, or ride a bike. Also encourage them to participate in more vigorous activities such as running, swimming, or playing games that involve kicking, throwing and catching, and striking.

- Make time to be active as a family—walk to a local park, ride bikes, or walk the dog together.

- Buy gifts that encourage physical activity, such as balls, bats, and skipping ropes. Have fun helping children develop and practice their skills.

- Park farther away from your destination (whether it is the school, a sports practice or sporting event, or a retail shop), and walk the rest of the way.

- Go outside and play every day, rain or shine. Remember how much fun you used to have jumping in puddles after it rained?

- Head for the nearest park, the swings, or the jungle gym after school.

- Spray paint boundaries on the grass to look like a soccer field, and then play a soccer (kicking) game.

Activities
for Learning
the Essential
Physical
Skills

CHAPTER

5

Motor development provides children with the abilities they will need to explore the world of physical activity. Motor development often has been defined as the process by which a child acquires movement patterns and skills. The research is clear that children develop motor skills during the early childhood years and that those who do not receive exposure to and instruction in skill-development activities may begin school with delays in physical development. There are many things that can influence a child's motor development, including genetics, body size and build, nutrition, and skill practice.

Skill development is important as children grow, so they can have the tools to stay active. No matter what the activity, a child cannot take part successfully if he has not mastered the essential fundamental movement skills contained within the activity.

What are the basic physical skills children need to live physically active and healthy lives? Acquiring physical skills is similar to learning the alphabet or learning about numbers; all children need to learn the basics and have a foundation on which to base future learning. When children begin school they learn basic skills in language. They learn the alphabet. They learn that letters form words; words form sentences; and sentences can be made up of verbs, adverbs, adjectives, and nouns. Children learn about numbers and then that numbers can be added, subtracted, divided, and multiplied. From experience and research, we know that children who do not develop a foundation of these basic academic skills are less likely to be successful in school.

We also know that children who do not develop a foundation of basic physical skills are less likely to participate in physical activities on a daily basis. Physical skills are invaluable lifetime tools that children and adults use to successfully participate in regular physical activity and to help maintain health and fitness.

So what are the most important physical skills you can help children learn? The basic essential skills are divided into eight categories:

- Traveling skills (walking, running, hopping, skipping, galloping, sliding, and leaping)
- Balancing

Encouraging Physical Activity in Preschoolers

- Jumping
- Kicking
- Throwing
- Catching
- Striking with body parts (volley and dribble)
- Striking with implements (paddles, rackets, or golf clubs)

A child who develops a strong foundation in each of these eight areas will have the skills to participate in a variety of games and physical activities for fitness and fun throughout life. They are not the only important skills, but they provide a good place to start. Help children gain these skills first, and then add others as the children show interest.

Most children naturally develop at least a minimal level of physical skills simply by moving through their home and school environments each day. But too many children never get the opportunity to refine these physical skills to a level where they feel competent to participate in popular games and physical activities. The activities that follow provide ideas for you to help children develop a foundation of physical skills.

Understanding Movement Concepts

In addition to learning how to perform basic skills, children also should understand *movement concepts*. Movement concepts provide specific cognitive information about performing a skill and help children move to higher levels of learning. Concepts help children understand how and where the body can move and the relationships body parts have to each other and to objects when the body is in motion. Movement concepts also relate to the quality of the movement, describing how a child should perform a skill. Movement concepts are divided into three categories:

- Space awareness
- Effort awareness
- Relationship awareness

Children's movements take place in space. For children to move safely and skillfully throughout their environments, they will need to understand how to move in the space around them.

Many times young children in school are seen as discipline problems because they frequently bump into desks and other children. Actually they may suffer from a lack of knowledge about space. A child who understands the concept of *self-space* is more aware of the movement possibilities available in the space immediately surrounding the body. *General space* is all the space a child can move in within the boundaries of the playground or backyard. When a child develops knowledge about self-space and general space, she will be less likely to bump into others and more likely to keep the environment accident free. Children must understand that they should not touch or get close to others when moving and that they should watch where they are going when moving through the space. Learning to move one's body safely in general space without bumping into others is a prerequisite to being able to move with equipment. For example, if a child does not understand general- and self-space concepts, she is not ready to hold a ball, racket, or bat in her hand. Safety first!

Space awareness refers to where the body can move. Concepts included are *general* and *self-space*, *direction* (forward, backward, sideways, diagonally, and up and down), *pathways* (straight, curved, and zigzag), and *levels* (high, middle, and low).

Effort awareness includes information on how the body can move. Effort includes the elements of time and weight. In terms of time, the child needs to recognize

Encouraging Physical Activity in Preschoolers

whether the movement is fast or slow. In terms of weight, the child should be able to distinguish whether the movement is done forcefully (such as striking a ball hard with a tennis racket) or softly (such as tip toeing across a room).

Relationship awareness considers with what or with whom the body can move. The initial emphasis is on the relationship of one body part to another. Children will begin to learn all the parts of the body, so they can balance and make body shapes such as round, narrow, wide, and twisted. In addition, children need to be aware of interactions with objects (over/under, on/off, near/far, in front of/behind) and other people (leading/following, working with a partner or a group) that will occur while participating in physical activity.

Understanding movement concepts is an important facet of skill development that goes beyond learning specific skills. The activities that follow provide examples of how movement concepts can be used to help children learn more about physical skills.

Now is the time to get active and start teaching children the physical skills we have been discussing. Get the equipment out, find a space to play, and have fun helping the children develop their skills.

Traveling Skills

Traveling, or locomotor, skills are the most basic skills that will make up a child's foundation of physical skills. These include walking, running, skipping, climbing, and galloping. Traveling skills help children move from one place to another. By age three, children are already proficient at walking, and by about age five they will have mastered other traveling skills. Skipping can be an exception, especially for boys, as some may not master the skill until around age eight.

Unlike many of the other basic skills that children need guidance and instruction to learn, traveling skills come naturally to most children. The best approach to introducing these skills to preschool children is to model the skills and perform the movements alongside them. When they need help, provide cues for refining the skills along with lots of practice opportunities.

Moving by traveling does not require any special equipment and is one of the best ways to get a child's heart moving faster and to use calories. Practice traveling skills for a few minutes each time children go outside to play.

Walking

Walking involves lifting and setting down each foot one at a time while moving forward but never having both feet off the ground at the same time. It is the basic mode of transportation for all children, and walking is the most popular form of physical activity for adults. The mature walking pattern is smooth with straight steps and with arms swinging in opposition to the feet. The child's head should be up so he can see where he is moving and can maintain balance when stopping.

WALKING— DID YOU KNOW?

A preschool child averages between 2,000 and 5,000 walking steps each day, depending on his activity level. Daily walking steps will increase as a child becomes older. Adults who take more than 12,500 walking steps each day are likely to lead active lifestyles; those who take less than 5,000 are more likely to be sedentary.

Marching

When music is playing, children often want to jump up and begin marching. Marching is an exaggerated walking step. The knees are raised as high as possible on each step, and the arms, with elbows bent, swing in opposition as in walking. By practicing marching, children develop a sense of rhythm while moving.

TEACHING POINTS

Marching—Children should raise knees high, bend elbows, and swing arms in opposition.

Use the following ideas to get started with marching activities. Children can practice in the school yard or backyard. You can also invite other groups of children and caregivers to march with you.

- Explain to the child that he is in a band and that the two of you are going to practice marching. Use two sticks to strike together or a drum to keep the beat.

- Move to the beat, emphasizing raising the knees high in the air each time the child takes a step.

- March at different speeds by beating the drum or striking sticks slowly or quickly.

- As the child understands the difference between slow and fast marching, add the cue related to the arm swing. You could say, "Bend your elbows and swing your arms high in the air."

- As skill improves, add obstacles to march around, and talk about marching in straight, curved, or zigzag pathways.

- Play some marching music and start a parade. Music with a consistent rhythmic beat is great for marching. Having a drum or two sticks to strike together would be great for making music.

Galloping

Galloping is an exaggerated slide step composed of a step and a leap. The front leg is lifted and bent, then thrust forward to support the weight of the child. The rear foot quickly closes to replace the supporting leg as the front leg springs forward again. Children begin moving forward by stepping on the front foot and bringing the rear foot forward. Children typically learn to gallop before they learn to skip. Although learning to gallop may appear to be easy, it does take some practice to master.

When you introduce galloping, ask the child to take a big step forward, keeping that foot in front of the body at all times. The child should start moving forward by stepping on the front foot and then bringing the rear

Encouraging Physical Activity in Preschoolers

Galloping—One foot is the leader, and the other foot follows behind.

foot forward. The next challenge is to gallop forward and backward, in different directions, and at different speeds. Children should try leading off from both sides—galloping by leading with the right foot and then by leading with the left.

Skipping

Skipping can be made easier for children if you model the skill. Skipping combines a hop and a step, first on one foot and then on the other. It is easier for young children to understand skipping if they are asked to first hop on one foot and then on the other. Hop and land on one foot, then hop and land on the other. Skipping is by far the most difficult travel pattern for children to master. Skipping is the first traveling skill children will encounter that involves bilateral movement—movement where each side of the body must do something different.

TEACHING POINTS

Skipping—Hop and land on one foot, and then hop and land on the other. Lift knees high.

It is not unusual to see children galloping before age four, but a child may be six, seven, or even eight years old before having a mature skipping pattern. As skills develop, ask the child to skip in different directions, in different pathways, and at various speeds.

Running

Running is the basis of most sport activities. The best way to introduce children to running is to take them outside and run with them. Mark off a course in the backyard or at the park. Place items such as balls, cones, or hoops throughout the space for the child to weave around. Start with a distance of 20 to 30 yards and add to the distance as the child is ready.

Encouraging Physical Activity in Preschoolers

Running—Bend elbows, swings arms, keep your head up to watch where you are going, and remain on balance when stopping.

Young children are easily distracted and want to look around a lot during running, so make sure they focus on looking forward instead of to the side or backward. Looking around may lead children to lose balance and fall. Start the children off running in a straight line, and then later have them practice curving around obstacles. At age three or four, running for thirty to ninety seconds without stopping is sufficient. Have the children take a rest and start again. Let the children decide how much or how little they will practice running. The point at this age is not to run a 3-mile race but to learn the mechanics of running and have fun.

Have you ever noticed how some children run faster than others? A particular child may have an efficient, smooth running pattern or may run flat-footed with his head moving from side to side and arms swinging all over the place. An efficient pattern suggests that there is arm and leg opposition, the toes point forward, arms are bent at the elbow and swing next to the body, and the upper body leans forward slightly. The best way to help children learn to run better is to ask them to run fast. Running at a fast pace requires children to use their arms and legs in opposition and to swing the arms for an efficient running pattern.

Running is a healthy and fun way to get exercise. It builds endurance for sports that a child may play later on in life.

Climbing

Climbing trees may be a fond memory for many adults, and children today also have the desire to climb. Beyond the fun factor, climbing helps preschoolers build strength and balance and is an excellent way for children to gain confidence in their physical skills. It is beneficial for preschoolers to climb trees or reach the top of a playground structure—

About 40 percent of all playground injuries are related to climbing equipment. More children are injured falling off climbing equipment than anything else on the playground.

and they will, whether you want them to or not! In children's eyes, trees, walls, and playground structures are there to ascend. Note, however, that experts such as the U.S. Consumer Product Safety Commission and Nemours, a nonprofit children's health organization, recommend that preschoolers be allowed to climb a maximum of 5 feet off the ground to avoid dangerous falls. At the preschool level, climbing can help develop muscle strength. Pull-ups and push-ups at this age are not appropriate as preschool children do not have the strength, coordination, or muscular maturity to do those activities. Pulling up with the hands and arms while climbing a ladder or playground structure builds arm, grip, and upper-body strength. Climbing also helps build leg strength.

Climbing—Provide guidance to make the activities safe and fun:

- Children should start with short, easy climbs. Adults should not lift or push; just be there to provide a hand if needed.

- Tell the children to move their arms slowly, grasp the bars or structure tightly, and move their feet slowly.

- Learning to climb down is as important as learning to climb up. Children should grasp tightly and move slowly. They should not jump down from a high level; instead, they should climb all the way down until their feet are on the ground.

- Talk with the child while he is climbing. Tell him where he might place his hands or feet if he looks like he needs help.

- Tell children to keep their hands higher than their feet and find safe holds to grab. If a child cannot figure out where to hold on, point out places for him to hold onto.

- If a child seems frustrated and asks for help in the beginning, look for small successes.

- At first, children need only a few minutes of climbing. Bring the child back to climb more when he is ready.

Children have a natural inclination to climb, and teaching them how to do it safely may help prevent an injury. Many sources list climbing as a traveling skill, but it is difficult to find instructional help for climbing. Unlike other traveling skills, climbing occurs in a vertical direction and therefore sparks safety concerns. Because children are going to climb, they can benefit from some adult guidance about the skill. It is preferable to have children learn about the forces of gravity from a knowledgeable adult rather than from an injury after falling. For some children, the fear of high places is enough to keep them from climbing too high, but supervision is a must for preschoolers.

If children are not interested or are scared to climb, do not push them. They will tell you when they are ready. If a child is timid about heights, let him hang around at the bottom of the playground structure. He will watch others climb and eventually will want to do it himself. Children with older brothers and sisters may be more willing to take on a playground structure. You cannot really stop a climber, and if you understand the benefits— building strength, balance, and confidence—you probably will not want to. Of course, you should allow a child to climb only to safe heights.

Beyond the Basics— Traveling Skills

For a child to develop the mature form of traveling skills, he will need lots of opportunities to practice. Chasing and fleeing activities can be a good option, and these skills are important for children to develop. *Chasing* (or following) is traveling quickly to follow, overtake, or tag a fleeing person. *Fleeing* (or leading) involves traveling away from a pursuing person.

Encouraging Physical Activity in Preschoolers

Leading and following—Use quick changes of direction (fleeing), and watch the hips of the leader to tell his next move (chasing).

Playing a follow-the-leader game lets children move in different directions and pathways using a variety of traveling skills; they also can build on cooperative play skills used when leading or following a playmate or caregiver.

Playing follow the leader is a prerequisite activity to playing tag games. Tag games using the skills of chasing and fleeing are, as children mature, used in a more elaborate form in sports such as basketball, hockey, soccer, and football.

Provide children with lots of opportunities to practice the skills of leading and following. If leading, the focus is to move in a variety of different ways and change direction often. If following, the focus is to watch the hips of the leader so you will know where he is going. In the beginning, move at a slow speed with the child and take turns being the leader and follower, then increase speed after children gain experience.

- Introduce the chase-and-flee activities to children by demonstrating the roles of the leader and follower. The leader's role is to move in different directions and pathways throughout the space while galloping, marching, and crawling. In general, the leader should challenge the follower to travel in a variety of different ways.
- The follower's role is to attempt to replicate the movements of the leader. The follower should not get too far behind the leader, and the

leader should be asked to slow down if he is getting too far away from the follower.

- About sixty to ninety seconds is sufficient time for a child to be a leader before changing places. Change the leader often.

- The caregiver should begin as the leader, moving about the space using a variety of different traveling movements and modeling the activity for the child. You might say, "Follow me and do what I do."

- Explain that you will take turns being the leader and follower. Give the child the opportunity to discuss and decide who will be the follower and who will be the leader.

- For safety reasons, suggest that you and the child not get closer than two giant steps from each other.

- Explain that you can move in different directions (forward, backward, and sideways) and pathways (straight, zigzag, and curved), as well as use a variety of traveling patterns and speeds.

- After the child has become experienced with playing this simple game, challenge him to be creative while leading and following around obstacles (over, under, around, and through).

Balance Skills

Balance may be the most important skill the child can develop because it is a required part of performing all other skills. Balance is required as an infant learns to crawl, sit, and stand, and as a four-year-old jumps to take off and lands without falling over. Jumping, running, throwing, kicking, climbing, striking with body parts and implements, and catching all require a child to be able to balance to accurately perform the skills. Balance is not only a physical skill but also is important for safety. Young children develop balance so they can walk without falling, ride a bicycle without tumbling down, or kick a ball without falling on their bottoms. Balance gets better with practice. It is widely accepted that good balance is the foundation for successful participation in all types of physical activity, including future sports activities.

Balance skills are task specific, suggesting that a child may do very well in one balance activity and not as well in another. Age is also a significant factor in performance of balance activities. As a child gets older, balance skills will improve in relation to growth and strengthening of the child's muscles and bones. A child's height and weight also influence balance skills. Although it may appear that preschool girls are better at balancing than boys, research suggests that gender has little effect on development of balance. Success in balance depends largely on age, experience, and practice.

Balance is commonly subdivided into two types, static and dynamic. *Static balance* is the ability to maintain a desired body posture or shape when the body is stationary. For young children, being on balance simply means not falling over. When a child balances on different body parts or in different body shapes, tries to stand on one foot, or hangs upside down from a playground structure, she is performing a static balance. *Dynamic balance* is the ability to maintain a desired body posture or position when the body is moving, starting, or stopping. When a child is skipping across the playground, walking across a beam, practicing a new dance, or running to kick a ball, she is performing dynamic balance.

Both types of balance require children to have control of their bodies. Children must develop balance to successfully participate in a variety of physical activities, but balance is also important to move safely in the home and play environments. For many young children, working on physical activities that require balance can be difficult. It will take time for children to be able to control their movements and learn different balancing skills. You can expect to see a wide range of balancing abilities among preschool children. Some five-year-olds, for example, will have better balance than others. Some may be able to excel in activities that require high levels of balance— such as gymnastics, biking, or skating—and others will not. Because preschool children tend to have rapid growth, their balance skills may appear more mature one day than the next.

A child's success in learning how to balance will depend on her understanding that the center of gravity must be over the base of support to maintain balance. All masses within the gravitational pull of the earth are subjected to the force of gravity; therefore, a center of gravity exists in all objects, including a child's body. The center of gravity is the point where an object's weight is concentrated. In a child, it always shifts in the direction of the movement or additional weight. If the center of gravity is stable and not moving, that is static balance. If the center of gravity is moving, as when a child is jumping rope or walking, that is dynamic balance.

The *base of support* is the part of the body that comes into contact with the supportive surface such as the floor, balance beam, or a grassy field.

Balancing—Children should use a wide base
of support, position the center of gravity over
the base of support, keep the muscles tight,
and extend body parts for balance.

The wider the base of support, the greater the stability will be. When initially working with a child to develop static balance skills, the activities should be designed to incorporate a wide base of support. For example, "Can you balance on two feet and two hands?" or "Can you balance on both elbows and both knees without falling over?" In both of these examples, participants will have a wide base of support because they have lots of body parts in contact with the base or floor.

Children are not going to develop balance skills unless they are challenged beyond doing activities where they practice balancing with a wide base of support. We must challenge children with situations where it is difficult to be on balance. The key for developing static balance skills is to place the child in an off-balance position and ask that she attempt to remain on balance. Place the child with a small base of support where the center of gravity is not initially over the base, and ask the child to remain on balance. For example "Can you balance on one foot for ten seconds without falling over?" or "Can you balance on one knee and one elbow?"

Beanbag Balancing

It can help young children to see something that is balanced before they try to balance their own bodies. An example makes the concept clearer. As an initial balance activity, have the children balance a beanbag on different body parts. In doing so, they create a visual and interactive demonstration of balance. The same rules of gravity exist with the beanbag as with the children. The beanbag must be centered on top of the child's body part, or it will not balance and will fall.

This is a great group activity; at home, parents and family members can join in. Give everyone a beanbag and get started with some fun static-balance activities. "Can you balance your beanbag on your head, knee, foot, back, stomach, elbow, forehead, and neck?" When the child is ready to move on to more difficult tasks, give her two beanbags and repeat the activities. "Can you balance the beanbags on your head and foot without letting them fall?" Ask if the child can balance a beanbag on each knee, on a knee and an elbow, or on each shoulder. The possibilities seem endless. You and the child can create your own combinations.

Encouraging Physical Activity in Preschoolers

Now add some movement and make this a dynamic balancing activity. Challenge the children with prompts such as, "Can you balance a beanbag on your head as you walk forward, backward, or sideways?" "Can you keep the beanbag balanced on your back as you move like an elephant?" "Can you balance the beanbag on your elbow as you slowly spin in a circle?" As the child gets the idea of moving while balancing one beanbag, add a second. Ask if the child can balance a beanbag on each shoulder while walking across the backyard. Ask if she can balance two beanbags on her back while moving like a lion. Participating in beanbag-balancing activities will help children recognize what balance is all about.

Body-Part Balancing

To continue your balancing adventure, challenge the child to balance on many body parts and a wide base of support and then progress to a few body parts and a narrow base of support. A large hoop placed on the ground provides the child with a space all her own where she can balance. If you keep several hoops on hand, children can invite their friends to participate, and they can each have space in a hoop. Ask the children to lay their hoops flat on the floor away from any obstacles that might be in the space. A child may find it easier to concentrate on the balance activity when the task is confined to the space inside a hoop. Challenge the child to hold her balance as still as possible for five to eight seconds or to freeze like an ice cube while balancing.

Prompt the child to balance with wide
bases and many body parts:

- "Can you balance on your hands and
  your feet?"
- "Can you balance on two hands, two
  feet, and two knees?"
- "Show me that you can balance on your
  head, hands, and feet."
- "Can you balance on your knees and
  your elbows?"
- "Can you balance on your knees and
  one elbow?"

Encourage the child to balance on narrow bases and few body parts:

- "Show me that you can balance on your head and feet."
- "Can you balance on one foot and one hand?"
- "Can you balance on one knee and one elbow?"
- "Can you balance on your head and one foot?"
- "Can you balance on one knee and one hand?"
- "Show me you can balance on your bottom. Try not to let any other
  part of your body touch the floor."

From these examples you and the child together can design other balance
challenges. Do not hesitate to ask the child for ideas about other body-part
balancing activities.

Encouraging Physical Activity in Preschoolers

HEADSTANDS

You may wonder when it is appropriate to help a child learn to do a headstand. This activity is safe for children who possess the muscle strength and static balance skills to perform the task. But many three-, four-, and five-year-olds do not yet have enough strength and balance to perform a headstand without help from an adult. Another concern is that most home-based care environments do not have gymnastics mats, which allow children to safely practice headstands. For these reasons, no instructions on how to do a headstand are included here. The skill is more appropriately introduced later in elementary school when the child has more strength and balance.

Initially, the child may have difficulty standing on one foot. To assist in skill development, ask the child to place one hand on a wall, bend one leg at the knee, and raise the other foot in the air. "Can you hold your foot in the air and count to ten? fifteen?"

Balance Boards

Balance boards are a good way for preschoolers to work on static balance skills. When a child initially puts her feet on the board, she is off balance and must work to redistribute her weight and gain balance. Children practicing with balance boards should distribute their weight equally with one foot on each side of the board and should hold their arms straight out to the side. To achieve balance, the child must find the best position over the middle axis of the board. The following activities provide some ideas to get you started. Remember that the intent of using the boards is to practice static balance. Children should practice balancing

Encouraging Physical Activity in Preschoolers

on the board and holding their balance without moving. This is a difficult challenge, as the boards are designed to place the child off balance.

- Stand and balance—Ask the child to stand on the board with feet spread apart and bring the board to a level position. Initially some children may place their feet too close together, and you will need to instruct children to place their feet farther apart for a wider base of support. Ask the child, "Can you stand on the board and balance, trying not to let the sides of the board touch the floor?" Then provide the cue for this activity: "Can you hold your arms out like airplane wings to help you stay on balance?" If the child has difficulty, stand facing each other, and help her balance by allowing her to hold onto your hands.

- Tummy balance—"Can you lie on your stomach and balance on the board? Try not to let your feet, knees, or hands touch the floor. Can you hold your arms out like airplane wings?"

- Sit and balance—Ask the child to cross her legs and sit on the board. "Let's see if you can sit on the board and balance."

- Knee balance—Ask the child to place her knees apart and hold her arms out like airplane wings. "Can you balance on your knees on the board? Be careful not to let your toes touch the floor."

Balance-Beam Activities

Besides static-balance activities, children need practice with dynamic-balance activities, which involve balancing while moving. Most children love to walk on balance beams (or on any object off the ground that looks like a beam), and they will frequently attempt to do so with or without adult help. At this age, a simple walk down the street with a preschooler could turn into an Olympic challenge as the child attempts to balance on every street curb and brick wall.

Introduce the child to walking on balance beams placed only slightly above floor level. Children should gain skill and confidence before moving to higher beams. The best starting setup is to use a beam about 6 inches off the ground. This is a height from which children can easily jump or step down without injury if they lose their balance.

Encouraging Physical Activity in Preschoolers

TEACHING POINTS

Balance beam—Children attempting to walk on a balance beam should extend their arms out to the side and look straight ahead, not down.

Consider the following tips for helping a child learn to walk on a beam:

- To begin, simply ask the child to walk along and balance on a chalk line drawn on the sidewalk or on a straight line of masking tape placed on the floor. Children should be able to walk along the straight line without losing balance and while keeping a foot on the line. As skill develops on the ground, move to a beam.

- Ask the child to step up onto one end of the beam and walk (not slide the feet) across it just as she would walk on a line on the floor. You can guide her by saying, "Step with one foot, and then step with the other foot." Initially the child may want to slide her feet across the beam, but encourage her to pick up her feet as she walks.

For safety, children should understand that the best way to get down from a beam is to jump and land on the ground on two feet. Even if the beam is only a few inches off the floor, it is still better for children to jump off the beam than to step off. Then, when beams are at higher levels, children will feel comfortable jumping off, reducing the possibility of injury from falling. Preschool children should never be on a beam higher than 10 inches without matting under the beam. Always remind children that if they feel they are going to fall, they should jump off the beam and land on two feet.

- You may need to hold the child's hand the first couple of times to provide confidence. Stand beside the child, not in front, while holding one hand. Standing in front of or behind the child may throw her off balance.

- It helps children balance while walking along a beam to hold their arms straight out at their sides. "What do you do with your arms when you walk on a beam? That's correct; you hold your arms out like airplane wings."

- Walking sideways on a beam may be easier for many children than walking forward. Ask the child to stand on one end of the beam with her arms straight out to the side. You can coach her by saying, "Pick up one foot and step sideways, then pick up the other foot and move it toward the first. Move your feet apart, together, apart, together." This is called a *slide step*.

- Walking backward on the beam initially will be difficult for preschool children. Because the child will not be able to see where she is going, she will fear falling as she walks backward. Just as in walking forward, walking backward requires children to pick up their feet and step. Suggest that the child walk backward and not slide her feet. Remember, arms out to the side.

Learning to Ride a Bike

If you teach a child to ride a bike, you open the doors to a lifetime skill that she can use to stay active. Take your time with this activity, however. Riding a bike takes an extraordinary amount of balance and concentration for a child to be successful. Wait until the child shows interest; do not force a child to learn to ride before she is ready. Most children will be ready between ages three and six, but there is no rush! The key guideline when teaching a child to ride is to keep it fun. If the young cyclist is not having fun, she will not want to continue biking. The best timing for learning to ride a bike depends on the child's physical development and when the child expresses an interest in trying to ride.

Other than the essential skills of balancing and pedaling, children should work on skills such as starting and stopping, riding in a straight line, looking

over their shoulders, and signaling turns. The better children are at riding, the less likely they are to crash.

Selecting a Bike Helmet

If you do not wear a helmet when you ride a bike, it is time to start. Children want to pattern what their adult role models do. Make sure the child understands the rule that if she is not wearing a helmet, she cannot ride the bike. Riding a bike is a fun way to get around, but bicycles are not toys. Bicycles are actually vehicles—a child's first one!

Make sure the helmet fits properly. Because preschool children grow quickly, check the size every six months or so. A bike helmet should be snug, level, and stable on the child's head. If the helmet moves a lot, it is too loose and needs to be tightened. If the child's forehead is not covered by the helmet, it is probably too small.

Encouraging Physical Activity in Preschoolers

Selecting a Bike

Selecting the right bike will be a key to the child's riding success. When you are buying a bike for a child, let the child help select it. Do not buy one that is too large, even though the child will eventually grow into it. Riding an oversized bike can slow down the learning process and can be dangerous.

What is the right size? Make sure that the child can stand over the top bar with both feet planted on the ground. She should feel comfortable and in control of the bike at all times. This is the best way to ensure safety. When riding a bike that is too big, children are more apt to lose control and crash. If the child is not yet ready for a bike with pedals, consider a push bike, which has wheels and a frame but no chain or pedals. A push bike can help a three- to five-year-old child coordinate steering and balance and help to transition to a pedal bike. A bike with training wheels helps the child balance with a wide base of support. When she is ready, the training wheels can be removed.

Learning to Ride

Choose an area where the child can learn to ride safely. Find a place that is traffic-free, large, flat, smooth, and paved. This location might be a driveway, park path, or empty parking lot. Empty tennis or basketball courts can also work well.

Remove the training wheels. Training wheels help children grow accustomed to sitting on a bike and using their legs to pedal, but they will not help them learn to balance. When the child is ready to learn how to ride, remove the training wheels. Also, remove the pedals using a wrench, and lower the seat. In doing so, you allow the child to sit upright with her feet flat on the ground. The goal is to help her feel more comfortable and steady as she begins learning to balance. Do not lower the seat too far. Young riders should be able to sit upright with their legs straight and feet on the ground.

The bike will roll more smoothly and the child will have an easier time coasting when bike tires are inflated to the correct pressure. Check the recommended tire pressure printed on the side of the tires.

Riding without Pedals

In teaching a child to ride a bike, emphasize balance first. You can add pedaling later. Instructions are as follows:

- Have the child begin by scooting on the bike without pedals so that she can get the feel of balancing it. This is a fairly easy process for most children, and she will easily figure out how to scoot so her bike moves along.
- After the child learns to scoot the bike, challenge her to pick up her feet and coast. Make it a game: Count to ten and see if she can coast with feet up for the full ten seconds. Gradually add more time as she gains confidence in her coasting skills. Do this on a flat surface first before adding a gradual downhill experience.
- Once the child has mastered the ability to scoot and coast the bike, she is ready to move on to turning and steering. Start with big, easy, looping turns. Use paper or plastic cups on the pavement in a pattern, and have the child practice steering between the cups.

- For more steering practice, draw an *X* with chalk on the pavement about 10 feet away, and encourage the child to run over it with the bike. This will help her to scan ahead and direct the bike to a specific target. As she improves, place a new *X* at 15 and then at 20 feet.

If the child consistently demonstrates all these skills, it is time to put the pedals back on the bike. Keep the seat in its lowered position, as the child still needs to be able to place her feet on the ground whenever she wants to stop.

Riding with Pedals

With the pedals back on the bike, teach the child how to start moving from a stopped position.

- Have the child stand over the bike with one foot flat on the ground and the other on a pedal raised and slightly forward (this would be the two o'clock position if observing from the right side of the bike).
- Coach the child to press down on the front pedal; this pressure will give the bike its forward momentum.
- Steady the child as she moves forward by placing a hand on her shoulder or the bike saddle, but let the child learn how to balance and feel comfortable on the bike without a lot of assistance.

As children get the hang of pedaling a bike, they can start practicing turns. Encourage them to do large circles and figure eights. Once simple turns have been mastered, try a more elaborate pattern.

Stopping the Bike

After practice on the push bike, the child should already be able to stop the bike by placing her feet on the ground. Now that the child is using the pedals, have her practice gently pressing on the coaster brake until she can use it without wobbling very much.

Be patient, as learning to ride a bike will take time for most children to master and refine. When the child is ready, find a bike trail and enjoy a two-wheeled family adventure.

Jumping and Landing

Children love to jump! And, they attempt to do so whenever possible. As George Graham noted in *Children Moving*, young children are fascinated by the task of propelling their bodies off the ground and momentarily flying through the air. Sometime around the age of two, children in your care will begin experimenting with the skill of jumping. By age three, they will be taking off, conducting short flights through space, and landing several dozen times each day. In this section we will discuss the types of jumping and will provide some activities for you to introduce to children.

Jumping is an important foundation skill and is used for many purposes. · Young children will jump to express emotion, curiosity, and even frustration. Jumping is also a skill that helps children get from one place to another, and it will be used in a variety of physical games and activities as children get older. Encourage children to practice their jumping skills often. It is helpful if you participate alongside the child in daily jumping activities. Remember that jumping can be exhausting for many children. After three to

JUMPING SKILLS— DID YOU KNOW?

The development of jumping skills in preschoolers tends to be about six months more advanced in girls than in boys. Yet boys tend to catch up with girls by age eight. Most children by that age will demonstrate mature jumping patterns.

Encouraging Physical Activity in Preschoolers

five minutes of jumping, children may need a brief rest period (thirty to sixty seconds) before continuing the activity.

There are five basic jumping patterns that young children should have frequent opportunities to practice:

- Two-foot takeoff to a one-foot landing
- Two-foot takeoff to a two-foot landing
- One-foot takeoff to a landing on the same foot (hop)
- One-foot takeoff to a landing on the other foot (leap)
- One-foot takeoff to a two-foot landing

Each of these jumping patterns requires practice to master the mature form. All patterns should be practiced frequently. However, in introducing jumping to preschool children, the first jumping pattern to be emphasized should be the two-foot takeoff to a two-foot landing pattern. If the child can bend the knees when taking off and landing, swing and extend arms when in flight, and successfully jump and land on two feet while staying on balance without falling, he will have a foundation on which to build other jumping skills.

Jumping patterns can be broken down into three parts:

- *Takeoff* is the action the child takes to propel his body off the ground. Takeoff always involves swinging the arms forward and upward, and bending the knees to help propel the body into the air.

- *Flight* is the action of the child's body while it is off the ground and in the air. There are some really neat things that a child can do while in the air. For example, he can make wide, narrow, or round shapes; wave; clap hands; or attempt to catch or throw a ball.

- *Landing* is the action of a child's body as it reestablishes contact with the ground. Landing requires that the child bend his knees to absorb the force of landing. You can tell a child that he is really good at jumping when he can land on both feet at the same time and stay on balance.

TEACHING POINTS

Jumping—Remember that using a cue word or phrase may help the child learn and perform a skill better. The following cues can help children develop skill in jumping off two feet and landing on two feet:

- Takeoff—Child bends knees and crouches body, ready to jump. Child swings arms forward and upward to take off from the ground.
- Flight—Child extends (swings) arms forward and into the air as feet leave the ground.
- Landing—Child lands with feet apart and body over feet. Lands softly and on balance without falling.

Encouraging Physical Activity in Preschoolers

Takeoff.

Flight.

Landing.

Activities for Learning the Essential Physical Skills

Hopping and leaping are variations of the basic two-foot-takeoff jumping pattern. In hopping, one foot is used to project the body into space, and then the landing is on the same foot. In leaping, the child will take off from one foot and land on the other, attempting to stay in the air as long as possible. The hop and the leap are more difficult than the two-foot jump because they require additional strength and balance, particularly when landing. Do not be too concerned if a child has difficulty hopping or leaping. Research suggests that only about 3 percent of five-year-old boys and 6 percent of five-year-old girls are at a mature stage of hopping and leaping. Practice these skills with the child when you have the opportunity, but spend the majority of your time working on the two-foot takeoff and two-foot landing.

Practicing Skills

As a child begins to learn the basic jumping patterns and gains confidence in jumping, he will need for you to challenge him with numerous practice opportunities so he can further refine jumping skills. Included here are ideas for additional practice. Set up a variety of jumping equipment. Create a fun area for practice by placing tape lines on the sidewalk to jump over; drawing circles and hopscotch patterns with chalk on the sidewalk; and supplying jump ropes, small wooden boxes, and small items to jump over.

Visual targets help young children practice jumping skills. A rope lying in the grass, chalk circles drawn on the sidewalk, and a row of hoops lying flat on the ground in a straight line all provide children with something to jump over and will help them learn and refine this new skill. Suggest that the children jump taking off from two feet and landing on two feet. Each time, emphasize one of the learning cues, such as beginning with the arms back and swinging the arms forward while jumping. The next time the child practices jumping, you can review the past cue and add a new one:

- "Make sure both feet get off the ground and land at the same time."
- "See if you can land on balance and avoid falling over."

- "Can you jump over the stick, taking off from two feet and landing on two feet?"
- "Show me that you can jump in and out of the line of hoops."

For most children, this jumping pattern will be practiced for several years before the mature form of the skill is reached. Remain patient if the child does not master the skill immediately.

Box Jumping

Another way to practice jumping and landing is to jump down from a step or off a small wooden box. Many children will have more success jumping down rather than trying to jump over an object because they have more time to get both feet ready to land at the same time. Young children should never be allowed to jump from a height of 10 inches or more. Their muscles and bones are simply not mature enough to withstand the force of landing from greater heights. The arm and leg movements for box jumping are similar to jumps off the ground. Instruct a child who is jumping off a box to bend his knees, place his arms back behind his body, and then swing his arms forward as he propels off the box. Emphasize landing on two feet and remaining on balance without falling over. It may help to place a mark

on the ground or lay a hoop where the child will be landing to provide a focus or target. A child who demonstrates fear or anxiety about jumping off a box should never be forced or required to jump.

As the child improves skills in jumping forward off the box and landing on balance without falling, he will be ready to try jumping backward off the box. Have the child practice on the ground first to make sure he is ready before he tries jumping backward off the box. Jumping backward is harder than forward, but the skill is basically the same. Bend the knees to get ready to take off, swing the arms, and land on two feet. The differences are that the back of the body goes first instead of the front, and the arms are swung from the front to the back. Ask the child to begin by placing his arms straight out in front of his body. Then he bends the knees and swings the arms to the rear, passing below the waist; the knees extend and the body propels itself backward into the air. Landing on two feet still should be the focus. Note that if the child is not able to jump off the box forward and land in a balanced position on two feet, then he is not ready to practice jumping off the box backward.

Encouraging Physical Activity in Preschoolers

Hoop Jumping

Young children need a focus when practicing jumping skills. A row of hoops lying flat on the floor in a straight line can help them concentrate on where to jump and land. If hoops are not available, use colored chalk to draw circles on the sidewalk as a jumping focus. Ask children to jump from one hoop to the next, taking off from two feet and landing on two feet. Remind them to swing their arms forward when they jump. Children should begin with both arms at their sides then behind the body and then should swing their arms forward as they jump.

Jumping Rope

Jumping rope has long been part of the culture of childhood. Even children as young as three can learn the movement patterns involved in swinging a rope and jumping. By the time they are five, most children can turn the rope and jump several times in a row. A 7-foot rope with plastic beads tends to work well. When children are learning, the initial pattern is to jump off two feet and land on two feet.

As children learn to jump rope, provide the following instructions:

- Hold your rope by both handles in front of your body with thumbs on top pointing down.
- Make sure that the middle of the rope is flat on the floor.
- Step over your rope.
- Bend your elbows up to your ears.
- Move your arms forward, and swing the rope over your head.
- Let the rope hit the floor.
- Jump over the rope; take off and land on two feet.

Safety note: In the initial stages of teaching the child to swing the rope and jump, ask the child not to jump while the rope is in the air. Children will sometimes do this and lose their balance. The rope should strike the floor in front of the child and be lying flat on the floor before the child jumps. Pushing off of two feet and landing on two feet helps children stay balanced when learning to jump rope.

Beyond the Basics—Jumping and Landing

As young children begin to get control of taking off and landing, introduce some of the following movement concepts to help refine and improve their skills:

- Practice jumping for distance—Ask the children to see how far they can jump, then use a tape measure to find the distance. Record the distance of the jumps.

- Jump and make body shapes in the air before landing—Ask them to make round, narrow, or wide shapes.

- Jump and turn in the air before landing—Instruct them to turn their bodies around one-quarter turn, halfway, or all the way before landing.

- Learn to jump over a small hurdle—Set up a hurdle no more than 10 inches high.

- Catch a ball in the air while jumping—While the child is up in the air, throw a ball for him to catch before landing.

- Throw at a target while jumping—Instruct the child to hold a small ball or beanbag in his hand, jump, and throw the ball at a target before landing.

Continuing to develop the basic two-foot takeoff and two-foot landing pattern will give children the self-confidence to continue to learn about and develop other jumping skills. Remember that jumping is a complex movement requiring a coordination of all parts of the body. Have fun jumping around the center or neighborhood!

Kicking

Many children's games include the skill of kicking. As soon as a child learns to walk and starts to run, around twenty-four months of age, she will begin experimenting with kicking. The running motion of the legs is a sign that the child has the strength to pick up one foot and swing it forward to contact a ball. By age three, children tend to be kicking balls everywhere.

Kicking is an activity that looks easy but requires a combination of different physical abilities—balance, movement, and timing. Be patient, as teaching a young child to kick a ball is harder than it sounds.

Kicking is really a unique form of striking with body parts. In kicking, the foot is used to strike a ball. Kicking requires that the child contact the ball with her foot while maintaining the balance necessary to propel the ball straight and far. When children practice kicking, the emphasis should be on development of the mature kicking pattern. Children develop this mature pattern by participating in activities in which they move their kicking leg through the full range of the kicking motion. Therefore, initial kicking experiences should emphasize kicking hard or for distance as opposed to kicking for accuracy. Activities involving kicking for accuracy are more appropriate for older preschool children.

For a punt, the ball is dropped and then kicked before it touches the ground. This is a complex coordination of body movements, as

Kicking—Guide children to practice the following actions:

- Contact the ball with the top of your foot (shoelaces)—not your toes.
- Contact the ball in the center.
- Place the nonkicking foot beside the ball.
- Eyes focused on the ball throughout the kick, not on the target.
- Kicking leg should follow through toward the target.

the child first must drop the ball accurately and then kick it before it touches the ground. A child commonly develops the movement pattern used in kicking a stationary ball well before she can effectively coordinate the actions of her arms and legs to punt. Some children initially will toss the ball instead of dropping it. Punting performance does not begin to improve until the child learns to drop the ball rather than toss it.

A 10-inch-diameter rubber playground ball or a foam or soft-covered soccer ball should be used for kicking. Do not use regulation soccer balls with hard coverings that may hurt a child's foot. This will discourage children from wanting to kick. Practicing kicking skills is generally an outdoor activity—a large grassy area is ideal.

When children initially practice kicking balls, it is natural for them to kick with their toes. The most efficient way to kick, however, is to strike the ball not with the toes but where the shoelaces would be. Children will not be able to control where the ball goes when kicking with the toes. Kicking with the toes happens when a child places her nonkicking foot too far behind the ball. The nonkicking foot is best placed right beside the ball so that when the kicking foot comes forward the ball can be contacted with the top of the foot or the shoelaces.

Kicking a Stationary Ball

Punch balls are excellent for children to use when first learning kicking skills. However, to use them you need a large indoor space such as a gym or an empty multipurpose room. Punch balls pop too easily outside and can blow away in the wind. If you do not have access to the space or do not have a punch ball, then a plastic beach ball, soft foam ball, or 10-inch-diameter rubber playground ball also will work.

This activity will give children the opportunity to practice the skill of kicking a ball as hard and as far as they can. The focus should be on moving the

OBJECTIVES FOR KICKING PRACTICE

Benchmarks for beginning kicking skills suggest that by the time a child completes kindergarten she should kick a stationary ball using a smooth, continuous running step and should demonstrate progress toward the mature form of kicking. This suggests that a kindergarten child should show progress toward understanding and being able to kick for distance.

kicking leg through a full range of motion. Instruct the children to not just tap the ball but to kick it hard.

- Ask the child to place the ball on the ground, take one step back, and kick the ball hard and as far away as possible.
- Have the child retrieve the ball and kick again.
- After the child gets the idea of kicking far, ask her to take several steps back away from the ball, then to run toward the ball and kick it.
- It may be helpful to place cones or markers out in the field to provide a direction for the kicking.
- Markers or cones can also be used to challenge the child to kick farther. Initially, place the cones about 10 to 12 yards away. You might

Encouraging Physical Activity in Preschoolers

Initial kicking activities should emphasize asking the child to kick the ball as hard as she can. This requires the kicking leg to go through a full range of motion from back to front and helps the child develop a mature kicking pattern.

say, "Show me how far you can kick the ball. See if you can kick the ball past the cones."

● As the child gets the basic concept of kicking far and hard, ask that she travel throughout the grassy area continually kicking the ball far and then running up and kicking it again.

Kicking for Distance

Place a traffic cone or something to mark distance about 10 yards away from the child. Ask the child to place a ball on the ground and step back about three big steps. Instruct the child to show you how far and how hard she can kick the ball. When the child can consistently kick the ball past the mark, move the mark back another 10 yards and repeat the activity.

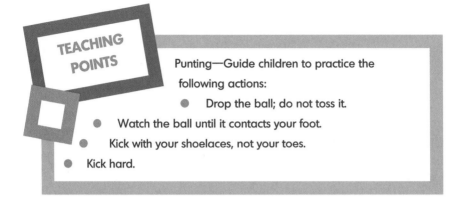

TEACHING POINTS

Punting—Guide children to practice the following actions:

- Drop the ball; do not toss it.
- Watch the ball until it contacts your foot.
- Kick with your shoelaces, not your toes.
- Kick hard.

Kicking for Accuracy

Set two cones or markers about 6 feet apart, and ask the child to stand behind a line 5 to 8 feet from the cones. Challenge the child to kick the ball so it travels between the cones. As accuracy improves, move the cones closer together and move the line farther from the target.

Punting

Most preschool children do not yet have the skills to be successful punting a football because the ball is simply too heavy and the children may not yet have the leg strength. Preschool children should practice punting punch balls or lightweight balls, practicing the motion of swinging the leg forward to contact the ball. You might give the following instructions to the child: "Hold the ball in both hands with your arms straight out in front of your

DEMONSTRATE PUNTING ACTION

Some children learn best by first watching others. When you are providing punting instruction, it may be appropriate to first demonstrate the skill to the child. You do not have to be a professional punter to do this. Children can learn a lot if they watch someone else perform a task, imitate that person, and then receive positive reinforcement for their efforts. Your punting demonstration does not have to be perfect, and the ball does not need to go far. You are demonstrating how to drop the ball and raise the leg to kick the ball.

Encouraging Physical Activity in Preschoolers

Which foot should the child kick with? She should practice kicking with alternating feet. When you kick the ball to the child, ask her to kick it back with a different foot from the previous try. Call out instructions: "Kick with the right foot." "Now kick with the left foot." You should alternate which foot you use each time you kick the ball to her as well. This will give her a visual reference model.

body. Release the ball so that it drops down and a little forward. Raise your kicking foot and kick the ball before it touches the ground. Make sure you kick the ball with the top of your foot. Kick it with your shoelaces."

Beyond the Basics—Kicking

After the child is comfortable kicking a stationary ball, start working on kicking balls that are rolling. Begin by rolling the ball to the child and having her run up to it and stop it with her feet. After she stops the ball, have her kick it back to you. Practice until the child can quickly stop a ball and kick it back to you with control. You will have a great time kicking the ball back and forth—you both get great exercise while the child learns and practices a new skill.

Throwing

Throwing is perhaps the most complex of all manipulative skills. *Manipulative skills,* or *object-control skills* as they are sometimes called, involve giving force to objects or receiving force from objects and most often are associated with games. Basic manipulative skills include throwing, catching, kicking, dribbling, volleying, and striking with a racket or bat. Because of the visual-motor coordination required in learning manipulative skills, they are more difficult for children to learn than locomotor, balance, or jumping skills. Manipulative skills develop through repetition and practice over periods of time.

It is almost impossible to take children for a walk in the park or along the beach without them picking up a stick, rock, or seashell, and throwing it into the air. Children love the feeling of propelling objects away from their bodies and watching where they go. Throwing is a required movement in

Encouraging Physical Activity in Preschoolers

Equipment for throwing could be lightweight foam, rubber, and plastic balls; old tennis balls; yarn and cloth balls; and beanbags. Items should be child sized and easily should fit into the child's hand. At the beginning stages of learning to throw, using an adult baseball or softball would be too hard, unsafe, and developmentally inappropriate.

many children's games. To enjoy and be successful in playing games, children must develop skill in throwing.

There are three basic throwing styles—overhand, underhand, and sidearm. No matter what the style, the basic learning progression remains consistent:

- An object to be sent away is grasped with one or both hands.
- In the preparatory phase, momentum builds for the throw.
- The actual propulsive phase—the release of the object—is performed.
- In a follow-through phase, the body maintains control and balance while using up the momentum of the throw.

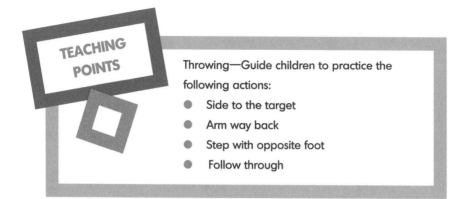

Throwing—Guide children to practice the following actions:

- Side to the target
- Arm way back
- Step with opposite foot
- Follow through

Overhand Throwing

Children need many opportunities to practice the skill of throwing overhand if they are to become proficient. Preschool children should focus on throwing hard at a target. This will enable them to go through the full range of the throwing motion. Follow these steps:

- Ask the child to pick up a beanbag or small ball and place it in the hand he is going to use to throw. (Allow the child to decide which hand feels natural for throwing.)
- Instruct the child: "Bend your elbow up and hold the beanbag behind your head. Step forward with the opposite foot, and throw the beanbag as hard as you can."
- If you are inside, direct the child to throw hard at the wall. If you are outside, ask him to throw as far (or hard) as he can into an open area.
- You may want to place cones or markers in an open area so the child has a large target to throw toward.
- Remember to stress "throw hard" and "step with the opposite foot."

The throwing skills of young children will vary greatly. Some children may want to get close to the target, while others will need the challenge of being farther away. Although this activity seems very simple, it is an important foundational, first-step activity for young children learning how to throw. If the child is having trouble stepping forward when he throws, place a tape line, jump rope, or chalk line on the ground, and ask that he step over the line when throwing. This will help him begin to develop the opposite-foot stepping pattern.

With young children, throwing activities should be both fun and success oriented. Research tells us that children need to be successful about 80 percent of the time to stay on task, to avoid frustration, and to have the best opportunity to develop skills. Children who consistently miss the target when they throw may get frustrated and not practice. The best beginning throwing activity is to simply ask children to throw hard. This allows children to naturally step with their opposite foot when throwing and assists in the development of a mature throwing pattern.

Having a target can help children direct or focus their throw. But do not be too concerned about whether or not a preschool child hits the target; establishing the throwing pattern is much more important. When young children become more interested in hitting the target than in throwing, by stepping with the opposite foot and following through, they may regress to an inefficient throwing pattern. Make sure targets are large and children are instructed to throw hard and far, so they go through the full range of motion to develop the mature throwing pattern.

As children get the basic concept of throwing hard while stepping with the opposite foot, use different targets to challenge them to keep practicing. Use large targets indoors, such as painting a target on a large sheet and then attaching it to the wall. Outdoors, provide a restraining line for the child to stand behind, and ask him to throw over another line that is 20 to 30 feet away. Provide a line that is closer if he cannot throw that far.

ABILITY AND PERFORMANCE FACTORS

If you work with young children, you will see a vast difference between the throwing abilities of boys and girls. Why is this true? Research suggests that with young children there is really no physiological reason for this difference. Skill in throwing is mostly related to experience and practice, and simply put, parents may spend more time throwing with their sons than with their daughters.

In addition, research suggests that the amount of time spent watching television is negatively correlated with throwing performance. Children who watch the most television tend to exhibit poorer throwing performance than children who watch less television.

So help children get plenty of practice!

Underhand Throwing

To eventually be able to catch a ball that is tossed in the air, a child will need to be able to accurately toss the ball upward. Do not worry about catching at this time; have the child concentrate on throwing the ball into the air.

Make sure you are outside in a large, open outdoor space. A yarn or foam ball or beanbag that will easily fit into the child's hand is best for this activity. Use a ball that will not roll too far away from the child. Instruct the child: "Hold the beanbag at your side, and move your hand upward and release the ball into the air. Throw as high as you can." Asking the child to throw the ball high into the air suggests to him that he has to throw hard, which will force him to go through a full range of motion with the throwing arm from below the hip to high into the air.

After the child gets the idea of throwing an object into the air, practice accuracy with underhand throws. Provide hoops or baskets as targets for practice (baskets should be large, at least 2 feet across). Stand about 6 to 8 feet from the basket target, and use the underhanded throwing motion to toss the beanbag into the basket. This time, take the arm below the waist and slightly behind the body before raising the hand toward the target and releasing the beanbag. Stress the cues "step with the opposite foot" and "follow through."

Punch-Ball Tossing

This activity will give children the opportunity to practice the skill of throwing or tossing a balloon straight up into the air. This tossing action will be needed later when the child wants to throw a ball in the air and strike it with a paddle or bat.

Encouraging Physical Activity in Preschoolers

A punch-ball balloon is made of a thick rubber or latex material, making it very durable. Punch balls move slowly through the air, so children have a better opportunity to track them with their eyes and then get their body in the best position for catching or striking. Punch-ball balloons should be inflated to a diameter of about 14 to 16 inches. The large rubber band that sometimes comes with these balloons should be discarded. Keep in mind that if preschoolers are playing with younger children, balloons should not be used with children younger than three.

Have children follow these simple directions to throw the punch-ball balloon straight into the air:

- Hold the balloon out in front of you with one hand on each side of it.
- Lower the punch ball below your waist so that it almost touches your knees.
- Raise both hands into the air and let go of the balloon as it passes your nose.

Timing the release is important. If the punch-ball balloon is released too soon, it may travel far out in front of the child, where it would be hard to catch or strike. If the balloon is released too late, it will travel behind the child and be impossible to catch or strike. Initially, you should encourage children to throw the punch ball only a few feet into the air. As the child develops skill, encourage him to toss it higher. When the child is ready, have him practice with different balls, such as a beach ball or rubber playground ball. As you will quickly see, the skill of tossing will help children succeed in the future when learning other skills, such as catching and striking.

Tossing beach balls is a great activity for a child with special needs because the ball travels slowly through the air. The slower speed provides opportunities for children at all skill levels to be successful. Children in wheelchairs can be successful tossing beach balls and catching them, but some may need assistance retrieving them. When using smaller objects such as beanbags or balls, choose brightly colored ones to help children with limited vision track them.

TEACHING
POINTS

Sidearm throwing—This skill is different from throwing overhand or underhand. When throwing sidearm, step with the same foot as the throwing arm.

Sidearm Throwing

The sidearm throw uses a different stepping motion than the overhand and underhand throws and may be confusing to a young child. Throwing a Frisbee is a good example of an across-the-body or sidearm throwing motion. The object is thrown across the front of the body while the thrower steps with the foot on the throwing-hand side. When throwing a Frisbee, the child should try to keep it flat.

Provide appropriate instruction to the child: "Hold the Frisbee so your thumb is on top and your fingers are on the bottom. Keep the disc lying flat like a plate. Before throwing, cross the disc in front of the body, then move your arm forward and release the disc out in front of your body."

Beyond the Basics— Throwing

Help the child take advantage of additional throwing opportunities:

- Throw at targets that are placed at different levels—high, middle, and low to the ground.
- Throw overhand and underhand at different targets.

Add some challenges to the throwing activities.

- Ask the child to see how many times he can hit a target.
- Ask the child to stand 10 feet away and see how many times in a row he can hit the large target on the wall.
- Set up a cone or marker 20 feet from the child, and provide ten beanbags to throw. Ask the child to try to throw a beanbag past the cone ten times in a row.

- Throw underhand by rolling a ball on the ground to hit a target (similar to bowling).
- Throw for height; for example, throw the ball over a net or as high as possible.
- Throw to a partner.

Each time you and the child practice throwing, remember that longer throws or hard throws to a large target help develop a mature throwing pattern. Always emphasize holding the throwing arm way back, stepping with the opposite foot, and following through.

Catching

A preschool child already knows that playing with a ball is fun. Some adults say a ball is the perfect toy. It does not require batteries, and you can play just about anything with it. By age three, children know about kicking and throwing and are on their way to developing those skills. Catching is a bit harder. Catching skills vary greatly at this age. Some children have learned to track the ball and get their hands ready and grasp the ball as it comes into the body. Others will need a lot more practice before they are able to play a game of throw and catch with adults or friends. Most children are not truly coordinated catchers until they are about ten years old.

Catching is receiving and controlling a ball. Children progress from catching a ball with their whole body, then with their arms and hands, and eventually with their hands alone. As children learn to catch, they may fear the ball at first and pull away to protect themselves. One of the reasons it is difficult for young children to develop catching skills is that they do not yet throw well. To independently catch a ball, the child must throw the ball into the air, find it in the air, track it with the eyes, and position the body and hands for a catch. Many young children just cannot combine all of these skills yet. How a child places her hands in front of her body is also important to success in catching. When a child is trying to catch a ball below the waist, she should place her hands with the palms up and the little fingers together. If the ball is above the waist, the palms should face upward and the thumbs should be together.

TEACHING POINTS

Catching—Guide children to practice the following actions:

- Keep your eye on the ball.
- Reach your arms toward the ball.
- Bring the ball into your body as it reaches your hands.
- Hold your hands with pinkies together if the ball is below the waist.
- Hold your hands with thumbs together if the ball is above the waist.

To catch or strike a ball, the child must visibly follow the ball with her eyes. Ball visibility depends on the color and size of the ball. Research suggests that the color yellow is a very high-visibility color. Children will be more successful in catching and striking when using yellow or other light-colored balls compared to using dark-colored balls. Imagine watching a baseball game or a tennis match using a black baseball or a dark blue tennis ball: The players would have a more difficult time tracking and thus would not be as successful at striking the ball with a bat or tennis racket. The size of ball you select is also important for development of catching skills. When a child is learning to catch in the preschool years, start off with a ball that is 8 to 10 inches in diameter. As the child develops more skill, smaller balls can then be used. Ideally, you should have balls of varying sizes and weights on hand for catching practice.

It is considered developmentally appropriate to select catching equipment matched to the size, confidence, and skill level of the child so that equipment assists the child in learning the skill and she is motivated to actively participate. Inappropriate equipment for learning how to catch, such as an official volleyball or basketball, leads children to frustration when they are unsuccessful, and thus they do not develop the skill. More appropriate equipment would include scarves, punch balls, beanbags, and a variety of sizes of lightweight balls.

Catching Using a Scarf

Initial catching activities might begin with a scarf. A scarf moves slowly through the air, giving the child plenty of time to track the scarf and get her hands ready for the catch. Scarves can be purchased or can be made from a 12-inch square of lightweight material. To begin, hold the scarf in the air above the child's head and drop the scarf. As the scarf slowly falls, instruct the child to reach into the air and catch the scarf. The higher you can throw the scarf into the air, the more time the child will have to practice tracking the scarf with her eyes and get her body ready to grab the scarf. Eventually the child will want to throw the scarf in the air and catch it without your help. You still can provide instruction: "Hold the scarf in your hand and down to your side. With an underhand throwing motion, raise your arm and release the scarf into the air. Throw hard so that the scarf goes high. Can you reach out and catch the scarf?"

Catching Using Punch Balls

Initial catching activities should involve the use of a punch-ball balloon (see equipment section for more information). The punch ball moves slowly through the air, giving the child time to track the balloon and get her arms in the position to catch.

To catch the punch ball, the child must first be able to throw it straight up into the air. You can provide the following simple directions to assist children:

- Hold the balloon out in front of you with one hand on each side.
- Lower the balloon below your waist until it touches your knees.
- Raise both hands into the air and let go of the balloon as it passes your nose.

Timing the release of the punch ball is important. If the balloon is released too soon, it may travel far out in front of the child, where it is hard to catch. If the balloon is released too late, it will travel behind the child and be almost impossible to catch.

As the child's hands touch the balloon, she should grasp firmly and bring the balloon in toward the body. Initially, the child may use her entire body to catch, but she eventually will learn to grasp with the hands only. Give the child a progression of punch-ball-catching activities to try:

- Drop the balloon, let it bounce, and then catch it.
- Throw the balloon into the air and catch it.
- See how high you can throw the balloon and still catch it.
- Throw the balloon into the air and see how many times you can clap your hands before you catch it.

Encouraging Physical Activity in Preschoolers

- Throw the balloon against the wall and catch it.
- Throw the balloon back and forth with a friend or an adult.

Launch-Board Activities

Coordinating throwing a ball into the air and then tracking the ball and getting the hands ready for the catch is extremely difficult for most preschool children. Most three-year-old children have no idea where the ball will go when they toss it into the air. Using a launch board is a fun way for you and the child to practice catching while eliminating the step of first throwing. A launch board allows the child to step on one end of the board, which then sends a beanbag or ball on the other end flying into the air directly in front of the child. This gives the child a good chance to catch the object without needing to be skilled at tossing it into the air.

The instructional emphasis for this activity should be to have children concentrate on getting their hands ready to catch the beanbag and to focus on watching the beanbag as it moves through the air. Children first should focus on attempting to catch the beanbag with both hands at the same time. Next, they should try with the right hand alone and then the left.

Instruct the child to place her beanbag on the low end of the board. She will then go to the other end, get her hands ready to catch by holding them out in front of her, raise her foot, and stomp on the end of the board. As the beanbag flies into the air in front of her, she will clap her hands around the beanbag and catch it.

As the child gets better at catching, other challenges can be added. These could be stomping on the board so the ball or beanbag goes higher, attempting to catch two beanbags at the same time, or launching and catching other items such as the child's favorite stuffed animal.

Catching with a Scoop

For this activity, you will need a large outdoor space. Scoops for catching can be purchased from toy stores or can be made from gallon plastic milk jugs. Cut out the bottom of the jug, hold the handle so the open end is facing up, and you have a scoop. Use a beanbag for this activity, as a ball may bounce out of the scoop.

In this activity, the child practices throwing a beanbag into the air and catching it with a scoop. To be successful, the child must toss the beanbag into the air in front of the body and then position the scoop

Scoops make catching easier so children who have difficulty catching a beanbag in their hands will be more successful. Children in wheelchairs may find it easier to catch with a scoop than with the hands.

to catch the beanbag. A sequence for teaching this activity would include the following:

- Hold the scoop in one hand and the beanbag in the other.
- Toss the beanbag straight into the air so it travels about 3 feet high.
- Move your scoop so that you catch the beanbag in the scoop.
- Practice catching the beanbag holding the scoop in one hand and then in the other.

Playing Catch

The first rule of playing catch with a child is to wait until she is ready to play. Playing catch can be very frustrating to a child if she is not successful. In fact, it would be better for the child's skill development if you started with a game of throw and roll. In this game, the child throws a ball to you, and then you roll it back to her to throw again. When the child is ready to play catch, start with a large, lightweight ball or even a beach ball. Have the child stand with both arms and hands out wide. Toss the ball to her and ask that she wrap her hands around the ball and bring it in to her body. When using a smaller ball, start with the hands cupped together with the palms of the hands facing up. The child's hands should be slightly below waist level. Next, stand only about a foot away from the child, and toss the ball into her hands. Gradually increase the distance you stand from the child when you throw the ball. Challenge the child to see how many times she can catch the ball without dropping it.

Catching skills are difficult for young children to master. Most children will be at least five years old before they are ready to throw and catch successfully with a partner. Do not add to the difficulty of the skill by playing throw and catch together before the child is ready.

Beyond the Basics—Catching

Consider using this developmental progression of activities to help children refine their catching skills:

- While both you and the child are standing, roll a ball on the ground and ask that she catch it (scoop it off the ground) with her hands.
- Hold a lightweight ball in the air and drop it, asking the child to catch it before it hits the ground.
- Ask the child to drop a larger ball and catch it. Demonstrate first by bouncing a ball and catching it yourself.

- Bounce a ball to the child and ask that she catch it. (This is easier for the child than asking her to catch a ball thrown to her.)
- Have the child practice catching a ball at different places around the body. Catch above the head, below the waist, and on the right and left sides of the body.

Striking with Body Parts

Striking skills are part of many games played by children and adults. Dribbling and volleying skills will help children learn to strike objects with body parts. *Volleying* is striking an object into the air using a body part; *dribbling* is hitting or tapping an object with the hands to cause it to bounce slowly. Although it will be several years before a child who is currently preschool age is ready to volley a ball over a net during a game of volleyball or to dribble a ball while being guarded in a basketball game, he can start learning the skills that will help when playing these and other games. By the time a child enters first grade, he will show progress toward achieving a mature form of striking skills by being able to continuously volley a punch ball in the air with the hands and with different body parts. He will also be able to continuously dribble a ball with one or both hands. Children with more advanced striking skills at this age will be able to dribble a ball, switching from one hand to the other, while slowly traveling forward.

When volleying, the child can use his head, elbows, knees, arms, or hands to strike. When using the hands, volleying can be practiced using underhand and overhand patterns. Striking an object with the hands includes controlling a ball in an upward motion, which is involved in skills

Striking with body parts—Guide children to do the following:

Volleying with the Hands

- Keep your eyes on the ball.
- Position your body directly underneath the ball.
- Strike the ball by extending your arms upward.
- Follow through in the direction the ball is to go.

Dribbling

- Spread your fingers and relax them.
- Push the ball down, with your fingers controlling the bounce.
- Dribble with your finger pads.
- Keep the ball below your waist.

such as the overhead volley in volleyball, and controlling a ball in a downward direction, which is associated with dribbling in basketball. Striking the ball with the hands is an advanced skill and requires coordination of the hands and eyes. The child must be able to track a ball, get the body and hands in a position to strike, and strike the ball in one motion at the correct time.

For most children, it is difficult to track the path of a ball as it moves through the air and then to move underneath it to get into a position to volley. In the beginning, the child you are working with may find it difficult to contact the moving ball.

Striking Punch Balls

Large punch-ball balloons, which move slowly and give children time to track and prepare to strike, are excellent for helping young children

With preschool children, volleying activities are best done with larger, lightweight balls such as beach balls. The lighter balls move slowly through the air, providing more time for children to visually track the balls and to get their bodies and body parts ready to strike. A heavier ball can be used for dribbling, which will require the child to push down harder on the ball to continuously dribble.

develop striking skills. Frequent practice will help children achieve the hand-eye coordination used in games involving these skills.

The first step in striking a balloon is to throw it into the air. If the child adheres to the following directions, he should be able to consistently throw a balloon straight up into the air:

● Hold the balloon in both hands, and lower the balloon so that it almost touches your knees.
● Raise both hands into the air and let go of the balloon as it passes your nose.
● Look up so you can see the balloon.
● When the balloon comes down, strike it back into the air with your hands.

Children should practice striking with one hand and then with two. In the beginning, just making contact with the balloon will be an accomplishment worthy of praise.

Remember that striking a balloon with the hands will be difficult for some children and may take some time. If the child is having difficulty tossing the balloon in the air, you can toss it for him or just hold the balloon above the child's head and drop it to him to strike back into the air. The child will not be able to successfully strike the balloon without visually tracking it.

Children need to practice two striking patterns with punch balls or beach balls—overhand and underhand. The underhand motion begins by placing arms and hands in front of the body with palms up. Ask the child to raise his hands and contact the ball with his fingers. It will be easier in the beginning to strike with one hand. It will take time for a preschool child to coordinate being able to strike the ball with both hands at the same time.

The overhand pattern begins with the child's arms and hands above the head with palms up and elbows bent. When the ball comes down, raise both arms and contact it with both hands. After the child understands the basic overhand striking pattern, ask him to jump when he strikes to propel the ball higher into the air.

Striking with the Head

A child naturally may want to strike the beach ball with other body parts besides the hands. Striking with the head, for example, will be a fun challenge. This activity requires him to track the ball, position his body under the ball, and then jump into the air at the appropriate time to strike the ball with the head. Prompt the child: "Can you jump and strike the ball with your head? Make sure you look up and watch the ball."

Add some challenges to the body-part striking activities. Ask the child to see how many times he can strike the ball without missing. By age five, most children can strike a ball into the air from five to fifty straight times. Also encourage some variations.

- "Can you strike the ball into the air five times without letting it touch the floor? ten times? twenty times?" "Can you keep the ball in the air by striking it each time with a different body part?"
- "Can you strike the ball into the air first with your hand, then with your head, then with your hand, then again with your head? Can you keep this pattern going?"

Striking with Other Body Parts

Learning to strike with the hands and the head is only a start. Striking with a variety of other body parts can be fun practice. The following prompts can be encouraging:

- "Can you strike the beach ball with your elbow?"
- "Can you use your knees?"
- "Can you strike with your shoulder?"
- "Which body parts can you think of to use to strike the ball?"

Emphasize that as the ball moves through the air the child should watch it and get ready to strike it.

Dribbling

Children love to bounce balls. Lightweight beach balls or rubber playground balls are excellent for introducing dribbling skills. Regulation basketballs are too heavy for young children to dribble successfully and can frustrate them and defeat their desire to practice. Suggest that the child dribble the ball by touching it only with his fingertips and not with other parts of the hands.

Ask the child to hold the ball in front of his body, drop it, and when it bounces up, use his fingertips to gently strike the ball back down to the ground. Instruct him to keep striking the ball down softly and see how many times he can bounce it without stopping.

Children who are successful bouncing a beach ball are ready to bounce a rubber ball. You will have to judge when the child is ready. Use the same instruction as when bouncing the beach ball: "Drop the ball, and when it bounces up, strike it down gently with your fingertips. You will have to push down harder than you did when bouncing the beach ball." Ask the child to experiment with standing in one place and striking the ball with one hand and then the other. If the child is having trouble striking the ball, go back to using the beach ball. The child will be most successful if he practices dribbling on a hard surface.

When the child can dribble standing in one place, challenge him to dribble while walking forward and then walking backward. You will be amazed at how quickly the child can grasp the concept of dribbling and how much positive reinforcement he will get from being in control of the ball.

Beyond the Basics— Striking with Body Parts

Use the following initial tasks and subsequent challenges for preschool children learning to strike with body parts:

- Strike a beach ball in the air. Challenge them: "Using your hands, how many times can you strike the ball in the air in a row?" "Can you jump

Encouraging Physical Activity in Preschoolers

and strike the ball in the air with your head three times in a row?"
"Strike the ball softly." "Strike the ball as hard as you can."

● Strike a beach ball so it hits the wall. Challenge them: "Strike the ball as
high as you can with your hands so it hits the wall before it comes back
to you." "Can you strike the ball to the wall ten times without stopping?"
Ask the children to alternate using underhand and overhand swinging
motions.

● Volley a punch ball. Punch-ball balloons move through the air slowly,
so volleying a balloon becomes a great partner activity for the adult
and child. Following your instructions, the child will hold one hand in the
air. As you strike the punch ball to him, he will move his arm forward to
strike it straight back to you. Challenge the child to see how long you
can keep the balloon moving back and forth between you.

- Hit a beach ball over the net. Set up a low barrier or net for the child to strike a ball over.

- Repeatedly practice with the same hand. Strike a ball down continuously with one hand, and then practice with the other. Ask the child to see how many times he can bounce the ball without stopping.

- Dribble continuously while switching hands.

- Dribble in different places around the body while not moving the feet.

- Dribble in different directions—while walking forward, backward, and in different pathways. Dribble around various obstacles, such as in a curved pathway around traffic cones.

- Change speeds. As the child dribbles, see if he can change the speed that he travels.

Striking with Implements

Many of the games that children and adults participate in for physical activity require skill in striking balls using implements. We use bats in baseball and softball, sticks and clubs for hockey and golf, and rackets and paddles in tennis and Ping-Pong. Developing skill in striking with an implement is extremely important to the child's future ability to participate in partner or group games and physical activities with parents, family, friends, and other peers.

Finding appropriate equipment to help children develop the basic swinging patterns for striking skills can be a challenge. Most striking implements (tennis rackets, golf clubs, hockey sticks, and bats) are designed for adults and

Encouraging Physical Activity in Preschoolers

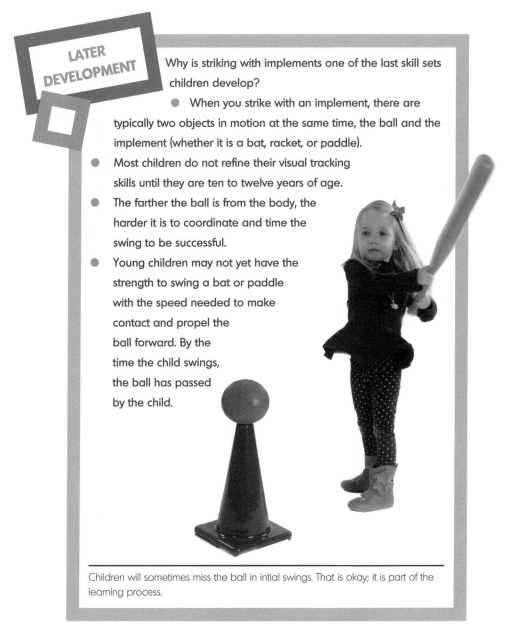

Why is striking with implements one of the last skill sets children develop?

● When you strike with an implement, there are typically two objects in motion at the same time, the ball and the implement (whether it is a bat, racket, or paddle).

● Most children do not refine their visual tracking skills until they are ten to twelve years of age.

● The farther the ball is from the body, the harder it is to coordinate and time the swing to be successful.

● Young children may not yet have the strength to swing a bat or paddle with the speed needed to make contact and propel the ball forward. By the time the child swings, the ball has passed by the child.

Children will sometimes miss the ball in intial swings. That is okay; it is part of the learning process.

older children and not for preschoolers. Search out lightweight equipment such as durable plastic bats, plastic clubs, and hockey sticks. Make sure the striking surfaces are large enough so the child will have some initial success in contacting a ball. Balls also need to be larger and lightweight for young children to be successful.

Remember that you are working to help children develop basic striking skills. Striking with an implement is complex and is usually the last set of physical skills a child will develop. Children must be able to accurately toss or drop the ball before they can visually track and choose the right moment to strike the ball. To be successful, children will need to put all of these movements together. They should be exposed to striking skills at an early age to learn the basic movement patterns. However, most children will not demonstrate the mature form of striking with implements until later in elementary or middle school, around ten to twelve years of age.

The closer the striking area of an implement is to the hand, the easier it is to make contact with the ball. With this in mind, introduce children to short-handled implements such as paddles or rackets before moving to longer bats, sticks, or clubs. When a child understands how to swing using a paddle or racket, she will have more success practicing with longer implements. The child also will be more successful striking with implements if she has first practiced striking with body parts (dribbling and volleying), because the implement serves as an extension of the child's hands and arms. A child will develop mature striking patterns only after lots of practice that takes her through a full range of the striking motion. So make sure the child takes a full, hard swing at the ball.

TEACHING POINTS

Striking with a paddle—Guide children to practice the following:

- Watch the ball as it moves toward the paddle.
- Make contact with the ball in the middle of the paddle.
- Do not move your feet when swinging the paddle.

Encouraging Physical Activity in Preschoolers

The basic action in all striking patterns is the same—putting an object in motion with a hit, punch, or tap. Striking with an implement calls on the child to coordinate several skills—tossing, tracking, and contacting the ball—into one smooth motion. At the same time, the child will be adjusting to the weight and length of the implement she is using.

Striking Lightweight Balls

Children should practice striking a stationary punch ball, beach ball, or foam ball before trying to hit a moving one. "Place your ball on the ground in front of you. Hold your paddle in one hand at your side. Swing your arm forward and smack the ball as hard as you can. How far can you make it travel?"

Ask the child to hold a ball out in front of her body, having one side of the ball resting on the paddle and using her free hand to support the other side of it. "Can you toss the ball high into the air and, when it comes down, strike it with the paddle?" If a child is having difficulty striking a ball tossed in the air, ask the child to wait until it hits the ground and bounces up and then strike it. Children by the age of five should be able to strike a ball in the air continuously eight to ten times without letting it touch the ground.

Striking a Stationary Ball

For many young children, striking a moving ball with a paddle may be difficult. Striking a stationary ball may be the best place to begin practice. You will need a short-handled paddle and a traffic cone that is at least 18 inches high or a tee to hold the ball. Instruct the child: "Place your ball on the cone. Holding your paddle, extend your arm to the side of your body and strike the ball as hard as you can." Remember that asking the child to strike hard helps her to swing through a full range of motion and will help her develop a mature striking pattern. This is called a *forehand swinging motion*.

The *backhand swing* also requires practice. Ask the child to face the cone while holding the paddle as she did in the forehand. Provide instruction: "Cross the paddle in front of your body and swing your arm forward, making contact with the ball." This swinging motion is similar to the arm action when throwing a Frisbee.

Long-Handled Implements

Most long-handled implements are designed for adults. For children to be initially successful, they need to use lightweight plastic implements for practice. Make sure the implement matches the size of the child and is the best weight and length for the child's skill level. Skills needed to strike with long-handled implements are among the last basic skills children will develop and are the most difficult. The difficulty a child may have in striking with a long-handled implement is directly related to the length of the implement. If you find that a child is unsuccessful with long-handled implements, put that equipment away for a period of time and use equipment with a shorter handle. Encourage the child to practice other skills and then come back to striking after a short break of several weeks.

Adults giving instruction should be more pleased with a child's improvement in swinging pattern than with the child's ability to actually hit a ball. Do not be concerned if every swing does not look the same. It is best for children to practice swinging hard at objects to swing through a full range of motion. This will help to develop the mature swinging pattern. Contacting the ball and sending it in a desired direction will come later after the swing develops.

Striking with long-handled implements—Guide children to do the following:

- Hockey swing—With your arms way back, watch the ball, and swing the stick forward, sweeping the stick across the floor. Use light taps if you want to keep the ball close to your stick.
- Swinging with a bat—Holding the bat back, focus your eyes on the ball, extend your arms and keep your swing level, follow through with the bat, and keep feet planted on the ground.
- Golf—Plant your feet shoulder width apart, and take a full circle swing with the club.

Safety should be of major concern when striking with long-handled equipment. Use soft, lightweight equipment, and make sure the practice area is free of obstacles and other children. The child will be focusing on striking the ball, not on where the bat or stick may end up. Make sure that no one is close to the child who is practicing striking.

Holding the Equipment

A right-handed child will hold her left hand on the handle end of the implement, and her right hand will grasp next to the left hand but more toward the striking end. The hand placement is reversed for the left-handed child. The child's thumbs point toward the striking end of the stick, and she will grasp it as if she is shaking hands with the implement. So while holding a bat up ready to hit a ball, the dominant hand would be on top, near the striking end. If the child is holding a golf club or hockey stick, for safety reasons the head of the implement is kept near the ground. With golf clubs and hockey sticks, the dominant hand grips under the other one, again toward the striking end. It is incorrect to hold the stick like a broom with thumbs toward the handle end. The child should never cross her arms when grasping the implement. If striking with a bat or golf-type implement, the hands should be close together. If striking to direct a ball in a particular direction on the ground, as with a hockey stick, the hands should be farther apart.

Encouraging Physical Activity in Preschoolers

Striking with a Hockey Stick

Striking with a hockey stick is an underhand striking pattern. The main idea in hockey is to keep control of the ball, not to see how far or how hard you can hit the ball. With this in mind, ask the child to tap the ball softly and keep it close, not hit it far away. Start by having the child strike a stationary ball. When it stops rolling, the child should strike it again and then progress to striking a ball that is moving. Ask the child to hold the stick so that the blade is on the ground, then bring the stick back and swing forward to strike the ball. When using this striking pattern, the child should keep the blade of the stick close to the ground and below the waist.

To hold a hockey stick correctly, the child's thumbs should point down toward the striking end.

Golf Swing

Swinging a golf club—even a lightweight, soft, age-appropriate club for a preschooler—requires a lot of space, making it an outside activity. Initially, the child should use a larger ball or a beach ball and should hit with a stick or club that has a large striking surface. Do not be concerned with where the ball goes; the child should focus on making contact. Ask the child to take a full underarm swing with the stick and strike the ball as hard as possible. Remind the child not to move her feet. Planting the feet about shoulder width apart will provide some stability when swinging and will help the child strike the ball farther and with more force.

Provide instruction:

"Plant your feet so they do not move while you swing. Bring the stick back and look down at the ball, then swing as hard as you can. Make sure to hold on to the stick so it doesn't slip out of your hand."

Striking with a Bat

When swinging golf implements, an underarm motion is most appropriate. A horizontal or level swing is used when striking a ball with a bat. A preschool child should begin by using a plastic bat to strike a plastic ball off a tee. The placement of the feet is just as important as the swing. Ask the child to place her feet about 2 feet away from the ball, shoulder width apart, with the toes pointed in the direction of the ball. Ask the child to imagine that her feet are glued to the ground; this will help her stay on balance and not fall over during the swinging process. Improper foot position places the child too close, too far away, too far in front of, or too far behind the ball and lessens her ability to successfully strike the ball.

A cone or batting tee that is about 3 feet high is best for initial practice. A right-handed child places the left hand on the lowest part of the bat handle and grasps the bat with the right hand directly above the left. Hand placement is reversed for left-handers. Provide instruction: "Hold the bat back and swing hard. Make sure you look at the ball when swinging the bat."

Celebrate progress when a preschool child can strike a ball off a cone or tee in the desired direction three out of five times. Some children then may be ready to have a ball thrown to them, but for most, striking the ball off a cone is itself quite an accomplishment.

Beyond the Basics— Striking with Implements

Consider the following initial tasks and challenges for preschool children striking with implements:

- Practice striking a punch ball or beach ball with a paddle. Strike the ball on the floor, strike it up and strike it down, and strike the ball forward against a wall.

- Place a ball on a cone and strike it with a paddle; always work on striking the ball far.

- Place a ball on a cone and strike it with a bat, aiming to strike the ball far.

- Suspend a ball from a string and strike it. Plastic balls with holes work well; you can thread a string or small rope through the holes and hang the ball from a tree branch or playground structure.

- Initial swings with a golf club should focus on making contact and sending the ball forward. As the child develops skill, emphasize striking the ball so it travels into the air.

In striking with long-handled implements, the emphasis at the preschool level is simply to make contact with the ball. Do not spend too much time on this skill if the child is having difficulty. Remember that striking with implements tends to be the last physical skill set that children develop. If a three-year-old is having difficulty with the skills, put the equipment away for a short period, then come back to the activities in six months and reintroduce the skills at that time. These activities should be fun. If the child is not successful, she will not have fun.

Youth Sports

The topic of youth sports often comes up when talking with preschool parents about physical activity and skill development. Clearly youth sports can be an appropriate place for children to get needed physical activity. During organized youth sports, children will learn and further develop motor skills. They also will get practice they may not get at school or home. But when should children begin, and what should parents look for in a good youth-sport program?

Although some youth-sport programs are designed for preschool children, most experts agree that youth sports are more appropriate for children older than six. Most children are between six and eight years old before they have developed and refined their skills to the point they can be successful competing on teams. Many preschool children can throw, kick, and run, but few have developed the coordination to do two of these skills at the same time. Also, most preschool children do not have the attention span needed to listen to coaches or to understand the rules for playing the activity. Usually by age seven or eight, children begin to developmentally understand what it means to take turns or compete on a team. Placing a preschool child in youth sports too early may lead to frustration and can turn the child off from sports and physical activity in the future.

If parents do decide to put their preschool children in youth sports, the emphasis should be on learning the basic physical skills and on having fun. Participating in games emphasizing competition (winning and losing) is developmentally inappropriate at this age. Preschool children do not

About 35 million children in the United States between the ages of five and eighteen play organized sports each year. Yet 70 percent of those participating quit by the age of thirteen. More than 90 percent of participants said they would prefer to be on a losing team if they could play rather than sit on the bench on a winning team. Parents might ask, "What causes kids to drop out of youth sports?" There are many reasons, but one of the top reasons given by boys and girls is that they were not having fun.

have the physical or mental skills to understand team play and winning and losing; they just want to play and have fun.

If a preschool child does want to play a sport, though, what is the right sport? One that the child finds fun and interesting. Allow the child some freedom to try different sports. Eventually, he will find the best sport for him.

If parents do decide to place a child on a youth-sports team, they should select a program that has the following characteristics:

- Focuses on skill development and having fun, not on winning and losing.
- Uses informal teams, meaning that the child might be with a different group of children each week when playing.
- Does not keep score or standings from week to week. The preschool child does not care who wins; he just wants to play and be around other children.
- Has simple rules. Most children develop the appropriate physical skills and the attention span needed to listen to directions and grasp the rules of the game from age six to eight. Before that, rules are meaningless.
- Uses developmentally appropriate equipment and modifies the size of the field. For example, two balls may be used on the field during soccer so players have more opportunities to kick. Another modification would be making the size of the T-ball diamond half the size of a baseball diamond.
- Does not have rules that exclude a child from playing, even if he did not come to practice.
- Limits the emphasis on wearing uniforms.
- Does not have end-of-year tournaments. Competition between teams should be discouraged.
- Allows boys and girls to participate on the same team together and allows equal play for all participants.
- Permits coaches on the playing surface so they can constantly show children where they should be on the field and provide direct feedback about skill development.

- Limits practices and games to no more than one hour a day and no more than two days a week.

- Has a short season. One game per week for six to eight weeks is plenty of time at this age.

- Limits awards or trophies. The reward is the feeling of satisfaction and fun received from participating.

- Selects equipment designed to reduce injuries. For example, T-ball is played with a plastic ball and bat.

- Makes reasonable accommodations to encourage children with disabilities to play.

Signing a preschool child up for a youth sport is not the end of the parent's role. Learning to participate with others and play fair are important lessons for a child to learn during youth sport activities. Physical-skill development should continue to be emphasized and refined. Parents of preschool children need to be actively involved when their children are playing youth sports by doing the following:

- Give your child emotional support and positive feedback. Continue to provide feedback about improving skills; continue to emphasize use of cues to improve skills.

Encouraging Physical Activity in Preschoolers

- Attend all games or events, and talk about them afterward. Congratulate your child for playing and having fun.
- Do not expect anything from your child beyond participation and enjoyment of the activity. If he is not having fun, he is probably not ready for organized sports.
- Model respectful spectator behavior; do not yell at officials, other parents, coaches, or children.

Whatever you decide about participation in youth sports, make sure your child gets an opportunity to be active and practice essential skills each day. Research suggests that participating in sports can have a healthy developmental impact on young children. The key is that the program be developmental in focus. However, some children may not be interested in joining a sports team. Parents should understand if their children simply are not ready or just do not want to participate. Children can still get their daily physical activity by participating in activities that do not necessarily require team competition.

Parents should not view a preschool sport program as though it has anything to do with the child eventually becoming an athlete. Preschool youth-sports programs should provide opportunities for activity, skill development, and fun. If one of these ingredients is missing, do not have your preschool child participate. To be beneficial, participation in sports must be a positive experience. Playing catch in the backyard or hiking in the woods can be just as beneficial to a child as participating in a preschool youth-sports program.

Moving
Forward

As you have discovered, providing physical-activity opportunities for preschool children is a fun learning adventure. But the adventure is not over. The young children you are working with will soon begin kindergarten and will further develop physical skills through the elementary grades and into young adulthood.

As children physically mature and improve their capabilities, they will no longer require such intense concentration to practice skills correctly. Movements will begin to appear more natural and fluid. Over the next several years, with continued practice and instruction, individual skills will become more automatic and children will be able to combine skills together. They will then have opportunities to feel more successful in game situations and more confident in everyday activities.

Moving forward, refinement of skills may require competent instructors with training and experience in working with children. Physical education teachers; soccer, T-ball, tennis, and basketball coaches; and swimming, gymnastics, and dance instructors all can play an important part in helping children refine physical skills. Instruction can come from many different sources once a child has a foundation of the basic physical skills.

Over the next ten years, children may begin to show interest in many physical activities, including a variety of youth sports. Sports clubs and teams can help children refine their physical skills, but remember that most children are not ready for team sports that involve high levels of competition until age eight or later. Team competition can hinder skill development if the child is not developmentally ready. Remember to encourage but not push children.

New opportunities lie ahead for you and the children in your care. Help them see the progress they have made and enjoy the knowledge and strength they are gaining. Congratulations on helping enthusiastic preschoolers master the tools that will enable them to be active and healthy now and in the future. Their adventures in gaining physical skills for life have only just begun.

References
and Resources

American Academy of Pediatrics. 2014. "Physical Activity = Better Health." *healthychildren.org.* http://www.healthychildren.org/English/healthy-living/fitness/Pages/Physical-Activity-Better-Health.aspx

AVG. 2014. *AVG Digital Diaries 2014.* http://www.avg.com/digitaldiaries/homepage#avg_dd_explore

CDC (Centers for Disease Control and Prevention). 2014. *Childhood Obesity Facts.* http://www.cdc.gov/healthyyouth/obesity/facts.htm

CDC. 2014. *Health and Academic Achievement.* Atlanta: GA: CDC.

CDC. 2014. *Physical Activity Facts.* http://www.cdc.gov/healthyyouth/physicalactivity/facts.htm

Council on Physical Education for Children. 1994. *Developmentally Appropriate Practice in Movement Programs for Young Children Ages 3-5.* Reston, VA: National Association for Sport and Physical Education.

Graham, George, Shirley Ann Holt/Hale, and Melissa Parker. 2010. *Children Moving: A Reflective Approach to Teaching Physical Education.* 8th ed. Boston: McGraw-Hill Higher Education.

McDonough, Patricia. 2009. "TV Viewing among Kids at an Eight-Year High." *Nielsen Co.* http://www.nielsen.com/us/en/insights/news/2009/tv-viewing-among-kids-at-an-eight-year-high.html

NASPE (National Association for Sport and Physical Education). 1995. *Looking at Physical Education from a Developmental Perspective: A Guide to Teaching.* Reston, VA: NASPE. http://www.shapeamerica.org/advocacy/positionstatements/pe/index.cfm

NASPE. 2001. *Guidelines for Facilities, Equipment, and Instructional Materials in Elementary School Physical Education.* Reston, VA: NASPE.

Nemours. 2015. *Playground Safety,* accessed March 19, 2015. http://kidshealth.org/parent/firstaid_safe/safe_play/playground.html#cat20889

President's Council on Fitness, Sports and Nutrition. 2015. *Facts and Statistics,* accessed January 16, 2015. http://www.fitness.gov/resource-center/facts-and-statistics

Spock, Benjamin. 1946. *The Pocket Book of Baby and Child Care.* New York: Pocket Books.

Tinsworth, Deborah K., and Joyce E. McDonald. 2001. *Special Study: Injuries and Deaths Associated with Children's Playground Equipment.* Washington, DC: U.S. Consumer Product Safety Commission.

U.S. Consumer Product Safety Commission. 2014. *Public Playground Safety Checklist,* accessed September 9, 2014. http://www.cpsc.gov/en/Safety-Education/Safety-Guides/Sports-Fitness-and-Recreation/Playground-Safety/Public-Playground-Safety-Checklist/

U.S. Consumer Product Safety Commission. 2010. *Public Playground Safety Handbook.* http://www.cpsc.gov/PageFiles/122149/325.pdf

Index

Encouraging Physical Activity in Preschoolers

modifying for disabilities, 149

paddles, 56, 75, 85, 138, 158, 162, 168

punch-ball balloons, 17, 69, 75, 127, 138-141, 144, 146-147, 152-154, 157-158, 161, 168

rackets, 66, 75, 85, 158-160

safety guidelines, 77-80

safety issues, 69

scarves, 75, 144-145

scoops, 76, 148-149

storage, 76-77

target boards, 75

throwing, 133, 139

volleying activities, 153

Ethafoam, 71

F

Fast foods, 10

Fats, 7-8

Feedback, 22, 26, 45, 50, 53-55, 172

encouragement, 55-57

positive and negative, 54-55

specific, 53

Fleeing, 96-98

teaching points, 97

Follow-the-leader games, 23, 97-98

Forehand swinging motion, 162

Friendships, 42, 60-62

Frisbees, 141

Frustration, 45, 54, 95, 135, 149, 169

G

Galloping, 3, 5, 11, 13, 41-42, 84, 87, 90-91

cues, 48

music and, 64-65

teaching points, 91

Games, 3-4, 81

Gardening, 4, 56

Gender differences, 14

jumping and landing skills, 116

throwing abilities, 137

General space, 86

Golf, 3, 158-159

Golf clubs, 67, 71, 85, 158-159, 164, 166, 168

swinging, 164, 166

Graham, George, 116

Grapes, 36

H

Headstands, 105

Health, 4, 21

Healthy lifestyles, 6-9

Hearing impairments, 23

Heart health

physical activity and, 4, 7-8

water and, 34-35

Hiking, 57

Hockey sticks, 71, 158, 164-165

swinging, 164-165

Hooks, 77, 158

Hoops, 72, 103-104, 123

Hopping, 84, 120

Hydration, 29, 34-36, 61

I

Illness, 9

Individuals with Disabilities Act, 23

Injuries, 77, 79

bicycle, 112-113

Music, 19, 55, 64-65, 88-90

Encouraging Physical Activity in Preschoolers

Recess breaks, 28
Relationship awareness, 85, 87
Repetition, 17-18, 41, 50-51, 60, 132
    disabilities and, 21-22
Rhythm, 64-65, 75, 88-90
Ropes, 23
Routines, 22
Running, 3, 7, 11, 13, 19, 30, 42, 62, 81, 84, 87, 92-93
    cues, 48
    teaching points, 93

S
Safety issues, 69, 98
    accidents, 79
    bicycle helmets, 112-113
    climbing, 94-95
    guidelines, 77-80
    injuries, 77, 79
    jumping rope, 124
    long-handled equipment, 164
    rules, 61-62
    running, 93
    space awareness, 86
Scarves, 75, 144-145
Schedules, 22, 59, 61
School performance, 8
Scoops, 76, 148-149
Screen time, 6, 15, 27, 56, 137
    and obesity, 10
    limiting, 64
Screws, 74
Sedentary lifestyle, 7-8, 15, 27
    and obesity, 10
    limiting, 64
Self-confidence, 4, 24, 54, 78
Self-control, 40-42
Self-esteem and music, 64-65

Self-space, 86
Shape America, 11, 28, 60
Shelves, 77
Sidearm throwing, 133, 141
Singing, 64
Skill development. *See* Motor skills development
Skill instruction, 39-47
    appropriate tasks, 44-45
    continual practice, 50-51
    encouragement, 55-57
    initiating activities, 43
    modeling skills, 51-52
    observing, 40-42
    providing feedback, 53-55
    refining skills, 45-49
Skill refinement, 45-49, 174-175
    defined, 46
Skipping, 3, 5, 11-12, 41, 84, 87, 91-92
    cues, 48
    music and, 64-65
Sleep, 8-9
    apnea, 9
Slide steps, 111
Slides, 77
Sliding, 84
Social skills, 60-62
Sodas, 35-36
    calories in, 38
    kicking the habit, 37-38
Softball, 158
Softballs, 17, 133
Space awareness, 85-86
Special needs, 76
    modifying equipment for, 76, 149
    physical activity and, 21-23
Spock, Benjamin, 39

Encouraging Physical Activity in Preschoolers